DEVOTIONAL COMMENTARY

THE
Dreamer

the path of favor

Brian & Candice Simmons

BroadStreet
PUBLISHING

BroadStreet Publishing® Group, LLC
Savage, Minnesota, USA
BroadStreetPublishing.com

The Dreamer: *the path of favor*

Copyright © 2021 Brian Simmons and Candice Simmons

978-1-4245-5955-8 (softcover)
978-1-4245-5956-5 (e-book)

All rights reserved. No part of this book may be reproduced in any form, except for brief quotations in printed reviews, without permission in writing from the publisher.

Scripture quotations marked TPT are from The Passion Translation®. Copyright © 2017, 2018, 2020 by Passion & Fire Ministries, Inc. Used by permission. All rights reserved. ThePassionTranslation.com. Scripture quotations marked NIV are taken from The Holy Bible, New International Version® NIV®. Copyright © 1973, 1978, 1984, 2011 by Biblica, Inc.™ Used by permission. All rights reserved worldwide.

Stock or custom editions of BroadStreet Publishing titles may be purchased in bulk for educational, business, ministry, fundraising, or sales promotional use. For information, please email orders@broadstreetpublishing.com.

Cover and interior by Garborg Design Works | GarborgDesign.com

Printed in the United States of America

21 22 23 24 25 5 4 3 2 1

*"Don't be afraid...Even though you intended to hurt me,
God intended it for good. It was his plan all along,
to ensure the survival of many people."*

Genesis 50:19-20

CONTENTS

INTRODUCTION

*It was like a dream come true when you freed us
from our bondage and brought us back to Zion!
We laughed and laughed and overflowed with gladness.*

PSALM 126:1–2

There is such great joy when our dreams come true. Like Mary, we may ponder and treasure a word or dream from God long before we actually begin to see it materialize (Luke 2:19, 51). But as we hold on to those dreams, they have the ability to carry us through the dark valleys of disappointment. Joseph did not go from having a dream to being a prince and ruler overnight. On the contrary, there must be a period of learning to trust, a season of faithfulness and testing. In that season, we learn not to give up on the promises or on our dreams.

On our way to seeing our dreams fulfilled, we encounter difficulties and trials that we never asked for or imagined along the way. And we find ourselves ushered into God's waiting room, the place no one likes to be. In the waiting rooms of life, it would be extremely easy to lose heart and to forget the dream that you carry. But if we forget our dreams, then it will only remain a dream and no more. We do not have to perceive seasons of waiting as a time of inactivity; instead, we can use them as a time of seeking the Lord for the next step forward.

The Hebrew word for *wait* can also mean "to be entwined." For it's in the waiting room that we begin to learn how to wrap our heart with his, combining our love for him with his love for us. And it's in the waiting room that we begin to understand that we can trust him against all odds. God never gives us a dream or a promise that he does not intend to fulfill.

The Lord can bring your dreams back around in an instant. Just try to imagine Joseph. He had these illustrious dreams, and then he went into exile. He didn't just have one waiting room experience; he had three. He waited at the bottom of a pit, faced enslavement under the tyranny of a ruthless regime, and was thrown into a dark, dirty dungeon. If he were here today, he could tell you all about the waiting room. But even after all that time Joseph never forgot his dreams. Instead he learned to swap his fear for faith, his pain for purpose, and his obstacles for opportunity.

Dreams have the power to set our lives in motion, to change our focus, to heal us, to save us, to impart knowledge to us, and change the course of our lives and history. Our Father in heaven does not slumber or sleep, but he works the night shift and says and does some incredible stuff while we're asleep. The whole of our society has been affected through dreams that may have appeared ordinary to others, but to the receiver who understood it, it wasn't ordinary at all. And as they meditated on those dreams, they released a whole new world of new discoveries.

Books are born, works of art created, incredible pieces of music composed, victories won, and miracles released through the power of individual dreams. Here are some of the things invented because of a dream: the sewing machine, the periodic table of elements, the theory of relativity, books by Robert Louis Stevenson, music by Mozart, Stravinsky, Bach, and others—and the list goes on and on.

Our problem all too often seems to be that when we get an amazing dream or prophetic word, we're tempted to say, *Lord, how in the world can this possibly happen to me? Don't you know who you're talking to here? Really! You're gonna do what? Through me?* But instead we need to be like Joseph, who identified with his dreams immediately and made them the passion for his fire for the future. When an amazing dream gets ahold of you, it can be a game changer for you.

For example, Martin Luther King Jr., the civil rights leader, had a dream of freedom for all, no matter what our skin color. His dream not only affected him and how he lived his life, but it affected all of us and changed history, releasing freedom and hope for others to carry on. And all because he refused to give up on a dream that seemed impossible to others.

What about you? What's the Father's dream for you? I (Candice) can remember one dream that I had while I was in high school. I dreamed that one day I would serve others and be a Peace Corps worker. I saw myself going off to faraway places, ministering hope and healing to those in need. But after graduating from high school and while finishing up college, it looked like none of that would happen. It was during that time that I met Brian and we were married. So I set my dream aside thinking that we would probably settle in our hometown, and that would be it.

Just when I had given up, the Lord remembered (as if he forgets) and resurrected his promise to me. A few weeks into our marriage, some missionaries at our home church challenged us to give our lives for the gospel and go to the ends of the earth to reach a forgotten people group. And we were not only able to reach a tribal people with the gospel, but we've also ministered in over forty nations. God places no limits on the dreams he gives us. His idea for my dream was much grander than my puny little plans.

May God give *you* dreams and fulfill your destiny!

Brian & Candice Simmons

> *To dream the impossible dream*
>
> "THE IMPOSSIBLE DREAM (THE QUEST),"
> LYRICS BY JOE DARION[1]

I

JOSEPH, TEENAGE DREAMER

Jacob's son Joseph was seventeen.

GENESIS 37:2

The story of Joseph, the teenage dreamer, is perhaps one of the most dramatic stories in all the Bible. It is full of intrigue and contains a plot that twists and turns its way to a beautiful ending. The Joseph Journey takes one from youthful zeal and dreams of greatness to despair, disappointment, and betrayal. This is the most incredible story of forgiveness that you will ever find in the Bible, aside from the story of Jesus himself. We promise you that it will touch you in the deepest places of your heart. It is a story of family intrigue. A story of dysfunction and drama that even some of today's families continue to grapple with. And the Scriptures do not hold back the gory details but disclose it all. At times, it's like reading a soap opera.

It is a true story filled with the emotions of jealousy, fear, hate, and ambitions run amok. It is the story of a father named Jacob, who loved his son Joseph above his other eleven sons. It is the wonderful story of Joseph, the dreamer, who never gave up on his dreams but carried them through years of heartache until their day of manifestation. The Joseph Journey starts with a seventeen-year-old boy and ends with a man who sits as a ruler and prince over all the known world of his day. What a very melodramatic climax to the conclusion of Genesis.

Joseph's brothers hated him for his dreams and for the favor that he found in life. As you read about Joseph's journey with all its ups and downs, think of your own life and the things that you, too, have faced. We'll study in vivid detail the way God the Father used Joseph's experiences to form and develop his character. God used every trial and tribulation that the enemy put Joseph through as part of his preparation and positioning for him to rule and reign.

At times, this story is breathtaking—full of suspense, intrigue, and mystery. More than other human biographies in Scripture, you'll be able to draw parallels between the life of Joseph and the life of Christ. So much of the world's history and hopes are wrapped up in this young man and his dreams. Yet he had no clue while he was living it. God was raising him up to be a savior for his family and for the world.

This is a story of how God prepares a man for great authority and privilege. A pit, persecution, and a prison will all find a place in the preparation of this deliverer and savior, Joseph. The Father doesn't waste the trials and tribulations that we face each day but uses them to makes us his deliverers and leaders. We, too, can emerge on the other end as mighty conquerors with Christ. When we know the love and favor of a Father in heaven, each trial can yield the pleasant fruit of integrity.

As we study the life of Joseph, we will see not only how God used the enemy's attacks to benefit him. But we will also see how others benefited from them. For the Father's ultimate plans were accomplished in the end. Life has pain, and life has pleasure. There will be suffering, and there will be glory. Yet the overruling hand of God is seen in this amazing account of Joseph's life and will be seen in yours as well.

LET'S PRAY

Heavenly Father, I know your blessing and your favor rests upon my life. Your goodness to me is everywhere around me. You have never failed me, and you are my one true friend. I ask, as I begin this journey, that you give me the spirit of wisdom and revelation to unveil your plan for my life. Put your dream inside my heart. Amen.

2

THE SECRET WAYS OF GOD

*Jacob's son Joseph was seventeen, and he served his older half
brothers, the sons of his father's wives Bilhah and Zilpah, helping
them watch over the flocks. One day Joseph went to his father with
a bad report about their behavior.*[2]

GENESIS 37:2

The story of Joseph gives away God's secrets. It reveals how
God raises up champions and deliverers. Here are just a few of
those secrets that you will find in the following chapters.

Joseph had to learn that *vindication is from God* (Romans
12:19). As long as we don't try to help God, he will honor us in
his time. God is not out to prove us right, but he seeks to glorify
himself and transform us, even in the midst of our rejection.

Joseph had *to be matured*. The lessons of Joseph teach us
that there is a thorough preparation time in our lives before God

promotes us. The enemy loves to sift us (Luke 22:31–32), but God will use it for preparation. In this world you will face challenges, but the Lord will reward you double for your trouble, turning it all around to prepare you for his call on your life. It's never easy to walk through to maturity. We all think we're more ready than we are. But our testing often reveals that we're not quite ready yet. Joseph had to learn to use authority with humility.

Joseph had to learn *to forgive*. Our hearts are so easily deceived (Jeremiah 17:9). We often think we have learned a lesson only to see that we have not. Forgiveness is a lifelong lesson that will test us repeatedly. It is a test that comes without warning. Our need to forgive exposes our need of love. Love is the highest spiritual achievement there is. It's our perpetual goal. Our lack of love justifies God's delays in exalting us. To judge another is the grossest form of self-worship. When we judge another, we are stating, in effect, *God is only working in me*. Forgiveness forces us to remove self-pity and personal hurt from our lives. Forgiveness places us on the path of promotion and greater favor. I (Brian) have learned that when I hold hurt inside my heart and cling to my pain, I hurt only myself. The liberation of my soul comes through freely forgiving others.

Let's see what we can learn from the story of Joseph. It begins long ago in a home and in a land far, far away.

A TROUBLED HOME

Joseph grew up in a troubled home. His father had two wives and two concubines. Besides that, Joseph had eleven brothers who were always stirred to jealousy and competition among themselves. And then there was Joseph's aging father. When Joseph was born,

Jacob was already old, ninety-one years old, to be exact. Joseph was the son of his old age and quickly became his favorite child.

And let's consider the name Joseph, given to him by his mother Rachel, who had waited and waited to have a child. The name Joseph means "May God add another." Naming him Joseph infers that she wanted another son. Perhaps that gave Joseph a measure of insecurity, knowing that he was not enough to be Rachel's only son but that she had to have another.

How would you like to live your life knowing that your mother was wishing for another to come and take your place? With a preoccupied mom, an aged father, stepmothers, eleven brothers, and one sister, their home life was in constant tension due to their clashing emotions. No doubt, the antagonism toward Joseph grew among his brothers over the years. We take up the story with Joseph at seventeen years old.

Let's Pray

My Father, I delight in being your child. Your favor and your grace have made me what I am. Your love was fixed on me before I was even formed in my mother's womb. Help me never to compete or compare myself with other brothers and sisters in Christ. I love what you are doing in my life, and you never make a mistake. Amen.

3

The Favored One

Israel's love for Joseph surpassed that for his other sons
because he was born to him in his old age.

Genesis 37:3

Being your father's favorite child may give you a lot of
self-confidence, but it also separates you from others in the family. Favoritism in a family breeds jealousy. To make matters even
worse, Joseph was also a teenage tattletale. One day, he told on his
brothers, bringing a bad report to their father. We can presume
he was not being malicious but simply wanted his father to know
what his brothers were doing. Joseph only wanted to be a faithful
son and please his dad.

Joseph's brothers (except for Benjamin who was a small child
at the time) were wicked. Reuben had committed adultery with his
father's concubine (Genesis 35:22); Judah committed fornication

with his daughter-in-law, who had disguised herself as a prostitute at the time (38:12–26); Levi and Simeon were cruel, having slaughtered the Shechemites (34:25–29). And ultimately all of them conspired to slay their own brother.

It's very difficult to understand how they could be sons of a chosen family, isn't it? They were all destined to be fathers of the tribes of Israel, but their hearts were so dark. But thank God! He knows how to transform our lives and make us into faithful sons and daughters of God.

Joseph was the favorite son, the son of Jacob's old age, the first-born of Jacob's favorite wife. Not only did Jacob love him most, but he also unwisely displayed it. And Joseph's brothers quickly realized that he was the one, the favorite son. It was only a matter of time before they unleashed their sibling rivalry.

The Jewish rabbis teach that Joseph was the servant of his stepbrothers, doing their dirty work (like a male version of Cinderella). None of his brothers knew it at the time, but Joseph was destined for greatness. He served as a shepherd, caring for the flocks. And up until he was seventeen, his chief duties were centered on the flock. With Jacob's wealth, there would be many flocks and many responsibilities in caring for them. That is, until Joseph received his new robe.

> Israel had made him a richly ornamented robe. When
> Joseph's brothers saw that their father loved him more
> than he loved them, they hated him and would not speak
> a kind word to him. (37:3–4)

Jacob made his favorite son a beautiful multicolored robe. This was more than just a pretty coat; it was the robe of a priest. Jacob did not honor any of his other sons in this way. By this act,

Jacob had designated Joseph the priest of the family.[3] No wonder jealousy consumed his brothers.

Can you imagine Joseph walking out to the sheepfold showing off his richly ornamented, multi-colored, ankle length robe? Joseph was one spoiled teenager. Wherever he went, others knew him by this intricately woven robe of many colors. Would he be able to work with sheep in a robe like this? I don't think so. This would be like a carpenter wearing a mink coat to the job site. No wonder it made his brothers angry. It's one thing to be favored but another to flaunt it.

Why didn't Jacob make a coat for Reuben, his oldest, or for Benjamin, his youngest? A garment like this was to be worn only by a prince. Jacob was showing his sons that Joseph was the mantle-bearer of the inheritance of the favored son.

You are a favored one. God has placed upon *you* a robe of revelation colors, the robe of righteousness given to you when you believed in Jesus Christ. How you respond to favor and blessing is the key to living for God. Will you take the Father's hand of favor today and live for him?

LET'S PRAY

My heavenly Father, what favor and blessing spills over my life when I come before you! The endless love you have for me is my strength in life. I delight in knowing you as my Father. Help me to take your right hand of favor and live in purity and light for your name's sake. Amen.

4

THE DESPISED DREAM

One night Joseph had a dream, and when he shared it with his brothers, they hated him even more! "Listen to this dream I had," he told them. "There we were, binding sheaves of grain in the field. Suddenly, my sheaf rose up and stood upright. Then your sheaves gathered around mine and bowed down to mine!" His brothers asked him, "Oh, so you think you're going to be our king? Do you actually think you're destined to rule over us?" So, the dream that he told them about made them hate him even more.

GENESIS 37:5–9

Joseph was both a dreamer and a prophet. Light and revelation filled this seventeen-year-old boy. His dreams enlarged his heart and released God's anointing over his life—such is the power of a dream! Although Joseph's dreams were truly from God and meant to bless his entire family, still his brothers hated him for it.

In his first dream, Joseph saw that his sheaf of grain was raised up over all the others while the sheaves of his brothers bowed to his (an obvious prophetic dream of what was to come in Joseph's exaltation). Joseph made a big mistake by sharing this dream. As it was with Joseph, so it is with us. There are times when it's unwise to share your dreams indiscriminately with others. They may not value what God is doing in your life and often misinterpret it as pride. That's exactly what happened with Joseph, and it almost cost him his life.

It's only natural to get excited when God speaks to us or when we get a wonderful dream about our destiny. But to take that dream or word and use it to affirm our gifts with others or to try to impress them shows that we are still immature. God is the One who confirms our calling and gifts. No one will fully appreciate the secret life you have in Christ. We selfishly want others to know it. But our need for admiration from others will always cause us to prematurely advance ourselves. God's wish is to promote us in his way and according to his timetable. But so often our immaturity refuses to wait for God's timing. Yet if we promote ourselves, God won't. Joseph's future imprisonment taught him that promotion comes from the Lord.

Joseph's brothers didn't need a dream expert to know the meaning of his dream. They got it in a flash. And this made them hate him more than ever. When we use revelation from God to show off, it only reveals that we desire to be honored by others. In fact, we will often reap the very opposite. Like Joseph, we may reap rejection.

Joseph was genuine and transparent; he was quite happy to tell his brothers his dreams. But Joseph's transparency lacked wisdom. Rather than thinking about how his dream could make his brothers feel or consider how they would react, he openly told it to them, causing them to turn against him. Always remember to use wisdom in sharing your dreams and revelation with others.

Most of us are like Joseph. We have a measure of gifting, a measure of anointing, and perhaps a true revelation that burns within us. Our gift may be real, but we are not yet ready for public promotion. We assume that just because God speaks to us that we're ready to run with it, but God knows best. He knows when we are untested, immature, and ministering out of a need to receive attention from others. Our wise Father will never reject us for these faults, for he knows this is our process of maturing.

The only way our life and our gift can operate in the fullness of Christ is when we surrender to his discretion and timing. It requires listening before speaking. Get ready for God to release you further into your destiny as he sees that you have been a good steward and are trustworthy. And as you obey, just watch your promotion begin to manifest.

LET'S PRAY

My Father, I love your wisdom and your ways. Teach me how to wait upon you. I don't want to promote myself or my ministry. I want to glorify you. Give me grace to learn the deepest lessons you want me to learn today. I offer you my heart. Amen.

5

The Misunderstood Dream

"Listen, I had another dream. This time, the sun and moon and eleven stars were bowing down to me." When his father and brothers heard it, his father scolded him, "What kind of dream is that? Do you really think that I, and your mother, and your brothers are going to come and bow to the ground before you?" So his brothers grew more jealous of him, but his father kept pondering Joseph's dream.

Genesis 37:9–11

We should all learn from Joseph's situation. Not only did he tell his brothers one dream, but he went on to share a second one and received the same response. When that happens, maybe we should ask ourselves, *Why are my dreams upsetting everyone?*

Joseph may have been operating in his gift, but his character had not caught up with his gifting.

His second dream was a confirmation of the first. And the number two in Jewish numerology is the number of witness. God was giving witness to the future destiny of young Joseph. Both dreams had parallel meaning: Joseph would be exalted over his brothers, his father, and his mother. The sheaves, stars, sun, and moon would all bow down to Joseph. But his entire family missed the true meaning of the dreams. They missed the fact that beautiful aspects of God's creation, the sheaves and stars, and not thorns and snakes, represented them in the dreams. Rather than Joseph simply being elevated above them, as the family believed, God intended for them all to receive blessings and anointing.

The sheaves of wheat are Jacob's sons, the Father's mature harvest on the earth, a ripened and harvested crop. And the stars represented his brothers. Stars are bright lights shining in the heavens. The sun, moon, and stars speak of God's heavenly people on the earth. Like Joseph's family, we so often see ourselves as ugly and unclean, not like stars and heavenly orbs. But we must remember that we are those on earth who have been chosen, washed, forgiven, filled, and blessed. Instead of provoking his brothers to jealousy, this dream could have brought them joy over God's mercy to them as a family.

The second dream speaks of government. God informed Joseph through the symbols of the sun, moon, and stars that he would receive government one day. In Genesis 1:15–18 we see that the lights of the sky were to "separate the day from the night" or "light from the darkness." Another interpretation would be "to govern." The "governing bodies" would one day bow down to Joseph and speak of the great authority he would have over his brothers.

If we would see the church from a heavenly viewpoint, we would not condemn those in the church who hate us. From the standpoint of eternity, God sees us all as sheaves full of life and stars full of light. Although the sons of Jacob were sinful, Christ still came through them (Matthew 1:1–3; Genesis 38:27–30).

Not only did he again tell his brothers his dream, but he also told his father. Joseph probably thought his father would be pleased; after all, he had given Joseph the rainbow-colored coat. But to his surprise, it had the opposite effect. Jacob rebuked Joseph and considered it a dream of fantasy, not prophecy. "His father scolded him, 'What kind of dream is that? Do you really think that I, and your mother, and your brothers are going to come and bow to the ground before you?'" But isn't this exactly what happened when they came before the ruler, Joseph, in Egypt? The jealous brothers would have no faith in Joseph's dreams, but Jacob, having been broken by God, kept the matter in his heart, for even Jacob had once received messages from God in dreams.

God wants to speak to you today through the story of Joseph. Will you steward the dreams he gives you? And perhaps the greatest question of all: Will you wait on God's timing for your dreams to come to pass?

LET'S PRAY

Eternal God, I love to hear your voice when you speak to me through your Word and through dreams. Tune my heart to hear all that you want to say to me. And give me grace to follow your direction, obey your Word, and yield my soul to you. I wait on you today to speak to me. Amen.

6

An Evil Plot,
an Empty Pit

*Joseph took off to catch up with his brothers and found them
at Dothan. As he was still a long distance away, the brothers
recognized him by his robe, and by the time he reached them, they
had plotted together to kill him. They said to each other, "Here
comes this dream expert. Let's kill him and throw his body into one
of these dry wells. We can say that a wild animal ate him. Then
we'll see how his dreams turn out!"*

GENESIS 37:17–20

Joseph's dreams really controlled and directed his life. This
dream of reigning burned in his spirit. How about you? What is
your dream? Do you realize that one day you will be raised up on
high and seated in the place of great honor and authority as you

reign together with your Lord? This is the vision that kept Joseph going through life and should be a comfort to us as well. He was to be a "sheaf" that didn't fall down. He was destined to be a sheaf full of life, destined to one day rule and to reign with Christ. If you had a dream about the stars of heaven bowing down to you, don't you think it might affect you too? Because Joseph saw himself as a star, he behaved accordingly. This is the key to understanding the next few chapters of Genesis.

In many ways, Joseph's life parallels the life of our beautiful Savior, Jesus. Christ was called a Shepherd in John 10:11 and the Shepherd of our souls in 1 Peter 2:25, so Joseph was also a shepherd. And later in his life, Joseph became the shepherd of his brothers and father, watching over their souls in Egypt. There is no one in the Old Testament who models Christ more than Joseph.

Notice Joseph's heart as he went to find his brothers. He truly loved them. But upon seeing him approaching their camp (for who could miss him wearing that coat?), his brothers began to conspire to kill him. They were tired of all of his dreams, and so they gave him the title of "dream expert."

His brothers scorned him for his gift. They couldn't endure the thought of bowing down to a brother more favored than they were. So rather than bow down to Joseph, they sought to kill him instead. And they said, "Then we'll see how his dreams turn out." They were like ferocious beasts. Not even the wild animals tear apart their own kind!

> When Reuben heard of this, he tried to save Joseph's life. "Don't take his life," he said. "No bloodshed! Let's throw him into this pit in the middle of nowhere, but don't hurt him." Reuben said these things because he planned to

return later to rescue Joseph and take him back to his father. (Genesis 37:21–22)

Reuben, the eldest brother, stood up for Joseph. He refused to be part of their murderous plan. Instead, he convinced them to throw Joseph in a pit in hopes of rescuing him later so that he could return him safely to their father.

But for some reason, Reuben was ashamed to use his authority to rescue poor Joseph. Are you like that? Are you afraid to stand up to those who would harm and slander the servants of God? Would you rather seek to be respectable in the eyes of others, even if it means leaving one of your brothers to suffer harm?

It doesn't look too good for young Joseph. They cast him into a pit, stripped him of his robe, and disgraced the favored son. This is exactly what happened to the Son of God. If God has destined you for greatness, it may get worse before it gets better.

LET'S PRAY

Father, you always know best. Your ways are not my ways. Help me to learn your ways from the life of Joseph. I know your favor is on my life and that promotion is ahead for me. Help me to submit to your process of growing me into the image of Jesus Christ. I will praise you for it, in Jesus' name. Amen.

7

A Pit on the Path to Promotion

*When Joseph finally caught up with his brothers, they seized him,
stripped him of his ornamented robe, his beautiful full-length robe,
and threw him into the dry, empty pit.*

Genesis 37:23–24

Joseph's brothers couldn't wait to get their hands on Joseph's robe. They hated that robe. Betrayals come against us to remove the favor-garment from us, making us a slave to our pain. But hope and love must prevail. If you will just remain faithful in a time of betrayal, you'll eventually be restored and wear the favor-garment once again. Betrayal is never the end of favor.

Joseph's life is really a series of robes: the robe of favor given to him by Jacob and taken by his jealous brothers, the stolen robe that Potiphar's wife ripped from him as he fled her adulterous advances, and the royal robe given to him for his reign in Egypt as God's savior for Israel. The coat of many colors had to go before God could use young Joseph. What is there in your life that you must relinquish before you can be set free to be God's instrument?

So now, Joseph's brothers throw him in a pit. And the only thing that was left for him to do was to pray. Maybe you are in that place right now. You may feel like you are in the pit or backed into a corner, and there's nothing you can do. But you can always pray. This is the time that we can get to know the Father like never before. There is nowhere else to turn. It's in these times that the Father proves himself to us.

> Judah spoke up and said to his brothers, "What will we gain by murdering our brother and covering up his blood? I have an idea! Let's sell Joseph to these Ishmaelites and not lay a hand on him, for he is our brother, our own flesh and blood." His brothers agreed… Joseph's brothers lifted him out of the pit, and sold him to the Ishmaelites for twenty pieces of silver,[4] and the merchants took Joseph far away to Egypt. (37:26–28)

When we're in a pit, we may convince ourselves that we're out of God's will. We are sure that God has forgotten us. But right when we think we can stand it no longer, God breaks through (Romans 5:6). That is exactly when Joseph's brothers lifted him out of the pit and sold him to the Midianites for twenty pieces of silver, the going price in those days for a handicapped slave! Nevertheless, going to Egypt was better than being left in the pit.

Isn't it amazing how the Lord sent the merchants from Midian at just the right time for Joseph? The Lord has ways to deliver us

29

that are beyond our comprehension. It is ridiculous for us to even try and figure out how God will pull it off. He just will! For Joseph, Judah sold him for twenty pieces of silver. Our Lord Jesus was also sold for silver, thirty pieces.

It is never good to sell our brothers. Whenever we devalue one another, we're selling one another; we are "shortchanging them" and not understanding their true value. How could a life be sold for mere silver? If Joseph's brothers had valued him as a sheaf or a star, as in Joseph's dream, they would not have sold him.

This is what happened to the Lord Jesus too. Because Judas did not view Jesus as precious and valuable, he sold him for thirty silver coins. And others have done the same to all of us. If they really understood the precious treasure within you, they would not have disregarded your life and value. May it be a lesson for each of us. May we never disregard or devalue another brother. Let's be careful not to sell our brothers.

Jacob, the deceiver, ended up being deceived by his sons. There was one more color added to Joseph's multicolored coat that day. It was the color of blood. The brothers dipped Joseph's robe in the blood of a goat and took it to Jacob as proof of his death. And it was the goatskin that Jacob used to deceive Isaac. Now it is goat blood that his sons used to trick Jacob. Joseph becomes a scapegoat for his brothers.

When Jacob hears the bad news, he tears his clothes and laments the death of his son. What grief and bitter pain come to Jacob, and he refuses to be comforted. There is no grief more painful than losing a child. "I will mourn for him the rest of my life, until I join my son in the realm of the dead" (37:35).

The next step in Joseph's journey was being sold as a slave to Potiphar. The favored son is now a slave to Egypt's prince.

Abandoned by his brothers, left at the mercy of merchant traders, yet God will never forget his spiritual seed. Joseph was simply going through the preparations for the day and hour when he would be reconciled to his family.

LET'S PRAY

> God of glory and wisdom, I come to you today. I place my heart and my hope in your hands. I long to be close to you no matter what my situation is today. Nothing will hinder my devotion to you. I pledge my life to you today. Amen.

8

FAITHFULNESS HONORED

*After the Ishmaelite traders brought Joseph down to Egypt, he
was purchased by an Egyptian officer of Pharaoh, the captain of
the guard, whose name was Potiphar. Yahweh's presence was with
Joseph and he became successful while living in the house of his
Egyptian master.*

GENESIS 39:1-2

The life of Joseph is a reminder that everything that happens to
us has the imprint of God upon it. If we will just wait long enough,
we'll see it. Joseph's betrayal by his brothers had now brought him
to Egypt, but God watched over young Joseph. He had arranged
for Potiphar, the military captain under Pharaoh, to purchase him
from the Midianites (Ishmaelites). Some Jewish historians believe
Potiphar was the chief of the executioners in Egypt. How's that for
a tough place to land?

When God anoints your life, no matter where you go, heaven's blessing will follow. God was preparing Joseph for ruling, so he was sold as a slave to one of the highest officials in the land. In this strange country, surrounded by a culture and language he did not understand, God prepared Joseph through testing. He had no idea that from the bottom of a pit he would be prepared to be the governor of Egypt.

"Yahweh's presence was with Joseph" (39:2). This is an amazing statement of the favor of God that was with this young man. God's very presence was abiding upon him. God's Spirit was forming this young slave into a future ruler.

When the Lord is with you, nothing can set you back. It may seem like time is wasting, and you're not getting anywhere, but God! God will have his way, and his will shall come to pass. Joseph may have been separated from his father and his brothers but not from God. Men can strip you of your coat of many colors, but no one can take God's sweet presence from you (Psalm 1; 139:1–12).

In the beginning, Potiphar had authority over Joseph, but after Joseph's prison experience, Potiphar and God gave him the place of rulership and authority. This is what it means to be prepared for ruling. Even though we may be prisoners now, we shall eventually become rulers.

Joseph had a God-favored life. The study of the life of Joseph is the study of the favor of God. He was faithful as a son, a shepherd, and a servant. He was diligent in all that he did. Wisdom guided him, even in a strange land, for everything he did prospered (Psalm 1:3). He not only adjusted to living in Egypt, but he also flourished in his exile, becoming the personal attendant (administrator) of Potiphar's affairs. Joseph never would have received such an honor if he had not demonstrated a high degree of integrity and faithfulness.

Potiphar knew what he was doing. Nobody had to tell him that God was with Joseph—he could see it. He knew that everything he possessed would do better in the hands of Joseph. He who was faithful over a few things was now being made a ruler over much (Matthew 25:21).

If Joseph had stayed in his father's household as the pampered son, he never would have learned the lessons of servanthood. His exile stripped him of honor and forced him to do menial tasks. But Joseph remained faithful until the favor of God promoted him.

Have you considered that some of the things you're going through right now might actually be the preparations by God for your next assignment? Many times, the things we learn from difficult situations teach us life lessons that we would never learn otherwise. God will always test his honored ones with servanthood before he raises them up to a place of authority. Before we have the ability to exercise authority, God will put us under authority so that we will learn the lesson of obedience and integrity in hard situations.

Yet even during our difficult seasons of testing and maturing, God is with us and will bless us no matter who may try to hinder us.

LET'S PRAY

Mighty God, thank you for living inside of me and protecting me every day. You are my strength, my hope, my life eternal. I come to you today for new power to live my life for you alone. I want to walk in triumph over all that may come against me today. I can do all things through Christ who empowers me. Thank you, my God. Amen.

9

SCANDAL

Now Joseph was strikingly handsome, very good-looking, and well-built. It wasn't long before his master's wife noticed Joseph. She demanded: "Come make love to me." "Never!" Joseph replied. "Don't you realize that my master has nothing to worry about with me in charge, for he has put everything he has under my care? There is no one greater in his household than me, nor has he kept anything back from me except you, because you're his wife. Why would I want to do such an immoral thing and sin against God?"

GENESIS 39:6-9

Temptation...Even though we have the power of Christ within, it's still possible for us to choose temptation over obedience. At the moment of temptation, we're making a choice to not walk in the Spirit but in the flesh. It's not that we're filled with a hatred of God; it's just that we ignore or purposely and conveniently forget him.

Instead of thinking clearly, we act on a hidden impulse that robs us of wisdom and prudence.

Temptation is an inevitable part of life on this planet. It may come, but the Scripture says that "times of testing [are] normal for every human being. But God will be faithful to you. He will screen and filter the severity, nature, and timing of every test or trial you face so that you can bear it. And each test is an opportunity to trust him more, for along with every trial God has provided for you a way of escape that will bring you out of it victoriously" (1 Corinthians 10:13).

Temptation is common to man, but we don't have to succumb to it because we have a way of escape, and that way is Christ because he's the only one who hasn't fallen into sin or yielded to its temptation. Through his virtue living within us, we can turn from sin's grasp and run away free as a bird. Evil is overcome with his good (Romans 12:21).

When Potiphar's wife saw Joseph, she only saw him as a servant of her husband. To her he was one she could command as her employee. As a fashionable officer's wife, she moved in social circles much higher than this slave. When Joseph rejected her repeated advances, it produced an unquenchable desire and eventually resulted in anger against the handsome Joseph. No matter how much our culture defends sex outside of marriage, adultery is wrong, cheap, and demeaning. It breaks the vow of the marriage covenant and changes a pure river into a sewer. What begins as attraction soon turns to poison.

Joseph passed the test and ran from the temptation. There are times when running is a mark of a coward, and there are times when running is the mark of courage. Joseph would rather have run in embarrassment than to take the chance of giving in and falling into the trap of sexual promiscuity.

First Thessalonians 4:3–8 tells us to run from sexual immorality. It's too dangerous to hang out with it. Run! To run from it is to be self-controlled, and self-control is a true sign of integrity. You will never reach the fullness of your destiny by disobeying God, especially in this area. Proverbs 25:28 says, "If you live without restraint…you're as helpless as a city with broken-down defenses, open to attack."

Samson was one who had no self-control and ended up under a pile of ruins, but Joseph exercised self-control and ended up ruling on a throne. It's better to lose a good coat than a good conscience. He lost his coat, but Joseph kept his character.

Joseph exercised a great deal of courage and determination to fight these kinds of battles day after day. After all, he wasn't an important leader that was out before the public and in view. He was only a household servant boy. As a slave, he had nothing to lose. Even if he did give in to temptation, he had no family nearby and no reputation to preserve. But Potiphar trusted Joseph, and so did God. The text simply states, "Joseph continually refused her advances and would not even go near her" (Genesis 39:10). Potiphar's beautiful wife could not entice him. He boldly said, "Never!"

You can say no to temptation as well, for the God of Joseph lives in you and will strengthen you each day.

LET'S PRAY

My kind heavenly Father, I ask for your grace today to always say yes to you and to the tug of the Holy Spirit on my heart. And I ask for grace to be like Joseph and say no when my heart is tempted to wander from you. May your love be the anchor of my soul today. Amen.

10

The Power of a Dream

*"Don't you realize that my master has nothing to worry about with
me in charge, for he has put everything he has under my care?
There is no one greater in his household than me, nor has he kept
anything back from me except you, because you're his wife. Why
would I want to do such an immoral thing and sin against God?"*

GENESIS 39:8–9

Joseph knew there was a high calling on his life. He knew
that his dreams were still unfulfilled. He was a man set apart for
greatness, and he was determined to keep himself pure because he
walked in the fear and awe of God.

There is power in your dreams. God puts dreams in our hearts
to give us a glimpse into our destiny. He uses the dream to test us,
to sift our hearts, and to perfect our character. Joseph knew that
he would be throwing away his destiny if he slept with Potiphar's

wife. There was no way he was going to give in to this temptation, even if it meant losing another robe. Now, let's take a look at the virtue expressed by Joseph:

1. Joseph understood the great favor that was given to him and would not violate the trust of his master. He valued that trust. When others believe in your calling and your vision, it should inspire you to rise even higher. To be loyal to God and the dreams he puts in our hearts means we won't surrender our favor to please the flesh.

2. Joseph looked at his own position and understood that he had been elevated to a place of honor; nothing was held back from him, and he had self-respect. One of the great sources of self-discipline and inner strength is to have self-respect. God's grace on your life means that you will honor who he is making you to be.

3. Joseph respected Potiphar's wife. "You're his wife" are words of love in operation. Though she was evil, he respected her, and Joseph was honorable toward her. A man of noble character will always be a gentleman. Joseph refused to take advantage of another man's wife.

4. His conscience told him it was wrong, and he obeyed. He knew that selling himself to this evil could hijack his destiny. The seventh commandment of the law had not even been given yet, but the ways of righteousness were already at work within him.

5. Because of her incessant advances, Joseph would not even come close to her (39:10). He knew where the temptation was and took action to avoid it. His resolution was strong.

6. The power of his dream kept him focused, pure, and determined. Your dream also requires you to keep your heart right before God. You may be closer than you think to your dream coming true.

7. Joseph understood the fear of the Lord. He knew that this "immoral thing" would be a sin against the majesty and glory of God. His thoughts were not only about keeping himself pure but also about holiness and the hope of his future. And he didn't just face this one day as she was determined to seduce him "day after day," for she refused to take no for an answer.

The fear of God always looks beyond the moment and sees the eternal God as the One we will stand before one day to give an account of our life. It will be our love for God alone that will preserve our soul as blameless in the end.

The Father's love within our hearts for our fellow man can conquer the seemingly irresistible desire of sexual temptation. It is a determined love that will not violate the rights and trust of others. Many people can maintain a certain moral standard of righteousness from the fear of being caught, but the Lord wants to be present in our hearts even when no one is looking. The strength of our love for God must be greater than any temptation. With a fear or holy awe of God in our hearts, we can look at even the strongest temptation, even realizing that no one would know or ever catch us, and still not want to sin against him.

The Lord has destined each of us for great things and has a work for each of us to do. So it should not come as a big surprise when temptations like this come. The devil seeks to destroy your destiny and rob you of the anointing. I thank God that there is a way out of temptation. It's not a secret, but it's hiding in his irresistible love. We must refuse to sell our hearts and inheritance for an adulterous affair.

Your heart will face tests, but you can resist. The enemy may come to sift you (Luke 22:31), but God will rescue you and raise you up for greater things. Remember, God can give us a love for him that is far sweeter than the love of another. It is a love that will remove loneliness and bring you into the pleasures of his right hand.

LET'S PRAY

Father, wash over my heart with your love, your glorious love. Go before me, prepare my path, and strengthen my heart. I want to live in the supernatural grace that you offer me today. With you, all things are possible. Amen.

11

FALSELY ACCUSED

"See! My husband brings this Hebrew foreigner here to make fools of us! He barged into my house and tried to have sex with me, and I screamed; and when he heard me scream for help, he ran out of the house and left his robe!" She kept the robe beside her until his master came home and she told him the same story: "This Hebrew foreigner you brought among us barged into the house and tried to violate me. As soon as I screamed out for help, he ran outside and left his robe here beside me."

GENESIS 39:14–18

The lust of Potiphar's wife turns to fury. And she despises Joseph so much for rejecting her that she uses his garment as evidence against him. With a trumped-up accusation of attempted rape, she takes the coat to Potiphar as a sign that Joseph had tried to seduce her.

If ever there was a time for God to reward Joseph, it would have been now. For day after day he had resisted her even when she grabbed him. But there was still a deeper work to be done in Joseph. Father God wasn't the one who threw Joseph in jail, but he did remain silent as Joseph was falsely accused and cast into prison. And all because Joseph was faithful to his master. He was helpless with no one to come to his aid. No one would believe him, especially not Potiphar.

Have you ever been falsely accused? Have you ever felt helpless and without defense? God had allowed Joseph to fall into an impossible situation, and the same could happen to us. He will take away our wiggle room until there is no wiggle left in us.

Those on the way to being used by God will, somewhere along the journey, experience being stalled in a placed of holding. This is how we reach to the heights of glory (1 Peter 4:14) and find our acceptance with God. We rightly expect to be chastened or punished when we do wrong, but it's very hard when someone holds us back or punishes us for doing right. However the Father at times allows this to give us the opportunity to taste of the nature of Christ (1 Peter 2:20–21; Philippians 2:5–11). You can be living the godliest life you can and still experience trials that will make you more like Christ. Moreover, we should remember that living a godly life does not mean that others will see you as godly. People may say the very opposite about you (like Potiphar's wife). This is the very ingredient God uses to grow us into him.

JOSEPH THROWN INTO PRISON

When his master heard his wife's account about how his servant had treated her, he became furious.[5] So

Joseph's master took him and threw him into prison,
the place where the king's prisoners are confined, and
he was left there. But Yahweh was with Joseph and
demonstrated to him his faithful love by giving him
great favor in the sight of the warden. The warden put
all the prisoners under Joseph's care; he was placed
in charge of all the prisoners and everything in the
prison. The warden had no worries about the prison
with Joseph in charge, because Yahweh's presence
was with Joseph and caused everything Joseph did to
prosper. (Genesis 39:19–23)

Joseph was cast into the king's prison, but God was there
with Joseph. This is another instance in which we can draw parallels between Joseph and Christ. As Jesus was falsely accused,
maligned, and crucified between two thieves, so was Joseph as
he was put between two criminals—the baker and the cupbearer.
Psalm 105:18 gives us additional information regarding Joseph's
stay in prison. "His feet were bruised by strong shackles and his
soul was held by iron." The last phrase can be translated "his soul
entered into iron," possibly meaning the inner strength of loving
and serving in a painful circumstance made Joseph's soul like iron.
He learned to serve and to rule over himself first before he would
be released to rule over others. The capacity to endure was working in his soul. With an iron will, he pursued God even while in
shackles. He opened his heart to trust the God who authored his
dreams and ordered his life.

Have you ever felt like you were confined in the King's prison?

LET'S PRAY

God, my King, I come before you today to thank you for the ways you have guided my life. Your path for me is perfect. I ask for grace, Lord, to follow you as close as I possibly can for the rest of my life. Amen.

12

WAITING WITHOUT BREAKING

The warden put all the prisoners under Joseph's care; he was placed in charge of all the prisoners and everything in the prison. The warden had no worries about the prison with Joseph in charge, because Yahweh's presence was with Joseph and caused everything Joseph did to prosper.

GENESIS 39:22–23

Can you imagine what it would be like to be thrown into prison for something you never did? Consider what prison life would be like. The conditions would most likely have been harsh, with little food and water, as well as continual physical, emotional, mental, and spiritual suffering for most of the prisoners. Yet God was with Joseph in his confinement. Heaven's favor and kindness

46

were evident, for Joseph was given the responsibility over everything that happened in the prison. Here are some likely duties that Joseph would attend to:

- Food preparation (if one was fortunate enough to eat)

- Cleaning up

- Emptying and cleaning the latrines

- Tending the wounds of prisoners

- Caring for sick prisoners

- Dealing with infestations of rats, lice, other insects, and rodents

- Watching over vulnerable prisoners

- Maintaining order and peace

- Keeping corruption at bay

- Dealing with death

- Ministering to the brokenhearted and the lonely

THE PRIORITY OF PEOPLE

God taught Joseph the priority of people before programs. He had to learn what it means to be his brother's keeper. A heart of compassion began to form while Joseph was in confinement. In the place of God's built-in destiny delay, Joseph embraced the depths of the Father's compassion for others. The lessons he learned of humility, wisdom, and love became the basis of his promotion. No doubt, there were days that Joseph struggled with the plans of God for his life, just as we do. But he remembered and persevered in his sonship regardless of his circumstances. God used the prison cell as the perfect crucible for his love to form in Joseph's heart.

Also, Joseph learned the heart of a servant in prison. It was crucial in his preparation, for he would one day be entrusted with so much power and influence. God chose to allow him to face confinement in a prison to teach him this lesson. He had the opportunity to show tender compassion to the other prisoners who were placed in his charge.

While in the dungeon, Joseph's anointing grew and grew. The iron of the shackles entered his soul and made him stronger. He was put in charge over all that was done in the prison house. Even in a prison, the most unlikely place, Joseph shined like a star. Even the prison warden recognized the extraordinary character of young Joseph. He was prospering again.

Psalm 119:71 says, "The punishment you brought me through was the best thing that could have happened to me, for it taught me your ways." Joseph is starting all over. This time it was at the bottom of an Egyptian dungeon. The prison was a school for Joseph, a place to build character, although unseen by others and forgotten.

Like Joseph, your life, with its setbacks and limitations, is being uniquely prepared for God's purposes. It seems impossible that your problems will be the source of your promotion, but watch over the next few years how God's presence is with you. Favor will increase and promotion will come as God deals thoroughly with your heart. The higher your calling, the greater your preparation. Get ready, a breakthrough is coming!

LET'S PRAY

My heavenly Father, you are wise, and you are good. Your plans for my life are the best. I yield my heart to you today for your Spirit to continue to make me like Christ. I give you my limitations and my delays. Your ways are always higher than mine. Give me a heart to follow your ways, no matter where it may lead me. In Jesus' name. Amen.

13

THE DREAM INTERPRETER

Some time later,[6] both Pharaoh's chief steward[7] and chief baker
deeply offended their master, the king of Egypt. Pharaoh was angry
with his two officers, so he incarcerated them in the same prison
where Joseph was bound. Then one night, they both dreamed. They
each had a prophetic dream with different interpretations. When
Joseph came to them in the morning, he saw they looked miserable,
so he asked Pharaoh's two officials, "What's wrong? Why the sad
faces?" "We had dreams last night," they answered, "and we have
no one to interpret them." And Joseph said to them, "God can
interpret your dreams! Please, tell them to me."

GENESIS 40:1-8 (CONDENSED)

Have you ever felt forgotten? Do you feel like God has put you
on hold for the rest of your life? What about all those dreams of how
God would use you? God will not promote us until the time is right.

God would not prematurely promote Joseph, not until he was ready. For now, he must learn the deeper lessons of the ways of God. It is through faith and patient endurance that we inherit what God has promised (Hebrews 6:12; 10:36). During Joseph's years of waiting, he held on to the dreams God had given him. But Joseph's destiny was more than ruling a household; it was to rule a nation. God used Joseph's prison time to create a deeper reservoir of grace. He was stuck in a place where all his natural talents and gifts that had been cultivated in him could have been rendered useless. The issue for Joseph was this: After learning to feed a household, would he be ready to feed nations and be a dispenser of life?

And then one day, Joseph met two important men in prison: Pharaoh's chief butler, or cupbearer, and the royal baker. They both were remarkably close to Pharaoh, knowing his business and overhearing his conversations. So why were they in prison? We don't exactly know, except that God put them there. They were in the very prison cell where Joseph was confined. What happens to the world is for the benefit of the church. They would become instrumental in Joseph's release from prison.

God has access to the spirits of men he intends to use for his own sovereign purposes whenever he pleases (Job 33:15). Each man, the cupbearer and the baker, had supernatural dreams on the same night. These dreams were about the future. They were prophetic pictures of what would soon happen to the two prisoners.

Little did they know that the young Hebrew man in prison with them was a master interpreter of dreams. God's Spirit gave Joseph hidden revelation and insights into the dream language of God. So he was able to give them the interpretation of what was to come. Joseph believed in the God who interprets dreams, and his confidence was not in himself but in the Lord, who gives dreams in the night.

It is wonderful when we dream, but it is far better when we seek the Lord for the interpretation. God, only God, can foretell the future (Isaiah 46:10). Man is shut out of that divine wisdom, except by the Spirit of Revelation.

The chief butler's dream was a prophecy of his happy release from prison in three days. Joseph was so convinced that God had given him the interpretation he tells the chief butler to remember him when it comes to pass.

It is interesting that Joseph could foresee their release, but he couldn't see his own. Most often, our prophetic gifting and words of revelation are for others, not for us. God has given us these gifts and designed the prophetic realm so that we can bless others and share the gift with them. When it comes to our own lives, we often have a hard time hearing for ourselves, which keeps us dependent upon God.

The chief baker's dream was a prophecy of his impending death. Both dreams and their interpretations were true. In three days' time, the cupbearer was elevated and restored to his former place while the baker was killed and hanged from a tree. Apparently, the cupbearer was innocent of wrongdoing, and the baker was guilty. To the cupbearer, Joseph brought restoration; to the baker, Joseph brought execution.

God used Joseph in his place of confinement, and God will use you to bless others in the not-so-perfect place you find yourself in. Heaven will flow through you when you seek to help others and put them first. This was a difficult lesson for Joseph but crucial for his preparation to rule and reign. Before you rise to rule, you must stoop to serve.

Let's Pray

Make me a servant, Lord. I want my life to be a blessing.
Help me today to lift my focus off my needs and be aware of
the needs of those around me. I will be your servant, God.
Keep teaching me these lessons so that I can bring glory to
your name. Amen.

14

GOD'S PERFECT TIMING

*The chief steward completely forgot about Joseph
and never remembered him.*

GENESIS 40:23

It hardly seems fair for the ones you help to forget you. It wasn't fair for Joseph. He interpreted the dream and prophesied the steward's release, but he was forgotten.

There was a man on the hill nailed to a cross next to Jesus. He asked to be remembered, and the Son of God took him to paradise. Jesus never forgets about us, but man does. No one remembered Joseph for a long, long time. He came into slavery when he was seventeen and soon afterward was cast into prison. And we know from Scripture that he was released from prison when he was thirty. That's a long time to be forgotten.

Even though the chief cupbearer forgot Joseph for a time, God did not. Perhaps like Joseph you've been let down by others who promised to help you but didn't follow through on their pledge. Don't despair, for God will never forget his children, even when others let us down. He remains eternally faithful to bring his plans to fruition in and to us. He will come at the appointed time just like he did for Abraham and Sarah as he told them in Genesis 18:14, "I will appear to you at the appointed time next year and Sarah will have a son!"

Forgotten for years, Joseph grew in character to become a prince before God and men. The early dreams of Joseph gave him no clue that he would face imprisonment, only that he would be exalted. It is next to impossible to predict how God will fulfill his word to us. We are convinced our destiny must be fulfilled a certain way, not knowing the process that we must go through first to get there. But when we have passed through a process that presents itself before us, he brings our destiny to life.

Perhaps your marriage may seem like your confinement. Or perhaps your job is your imprisonment. No matter what it is that you face, the Father is faithful to use the process and pressure in our lives to form Christ within our personalities even though we may not see or understand what is happening. And even though we know it, we often do not see how our circumstances could possibly be working for good. But the Lord sees the final product and knows how to use the process. As the apostle Paul says, "So we are convinced that every detail of our lives is continually woven together to fit into God's perfect plan of bringing good into our lives, for we are his lovers who have been called to fulfill his designed purpose" (Romans 8:28).

The enemy may be trying to crush you, but the Lord is busy making diamonds in the process. He is making us into his image.

The Lord does not always stop the process or the imprisonment when we think that it should end. But it will eventually come to an end as we purpose in our hearts to keep moving forward in faith and to not take offense at him.

In the meantime, others may see you in your imprisonment and conclude that God has forgotten you or that you will never be released to rule. However, in due time, you will advance and fulfill the very words God has spoken into your spirit. *Wait, young Joseph, just wait!*

How to Enjoy Your Time in "Prison"

1. Realize that the throne is coming, but it doesn't immediately follow the vision of your destiny.

2. Between your dream and its fulfillment, you will probably have some suffering, testing, betrayal, and delay, but God is still with you and will never forsake you.

3. Don't doubt in the dark what God has shown you in the light. His promises to you are still true.

4. Like Joseph, God will use you in your years of process and time of waiting. He will use it to school you for ruling if you let him.

5. Be prepared for those you help the most to forget you. But remember that the One who loves you most will never forget you.

6. Every suffering is preparation for ruling on a throne (Revelation 3:21).

7. Don't allow your vision to be your stumbling block. You may be bewildered at why God has not fulfilled the vision he gave you.

LET'S PRAY

God, I'm always surprised by the ways you lead and direct my steps. Today, I want to be surprised by your grace. Help me to walk in step with you today, no matter how strange it may seem. I trust you, my Father. In Jesus' name. Amen.

15

FROM PRISON
TO THE PALACE

*The next morning, [Pharaoh's] spirit was agitated, so he called
for all the magicians and wise men in Egypt. Pharaoh recounted
his [two] dreams to them, but no one could give him the
interpretation. When the chief steward heard about the dreams he
remembered Joseph and said to Pharaoh… "Once, when Pharaoh
was angry with his servants, he incarcerated me and the chief
baker in prison. We both had dreams on the same night but with
different meanings. There was a young Hebrew man imprisoned
with us. And when we told him our dreams, he interpreted them
and told each of us their meaning. And it happened just as he said.
Pharaoh restored me to my post, but he had the baker impaled."
After hearing this, Pharaoh immediately sent for Joseph. They
rushed him out of the dungeon to prepare him to meet with the*

king. When he had shaved and changed his clothes, he came and stood before Pharaoh. [He] said to Joseph, "I have had two dreams that no one can explain. I have heard that you are able to interpret a dream the moment you hear it." Joseph replied, "I cannot do it alone, but God will help me to give you the interpretation."

GENESIS 41:8–16 (CONDENSED)

Joseph had waited so long! He had asked the chief butler to remember him and to speak well of him to Pharaoh, but the chief butler had forgotten all about him. But there was an appointed time. Like Joseph, there is a set time for your deliverance as well. We must wait for God to move (Psalm 13:1; Habakkuk 2:3).

Pharaoh had two supernatural dreams that no one could interpret. And so it was Joseph's gift of interpreting dreams that brought him out of the prison. And it was also Joseph's dreams that landed him in prison in the first place. The wisdom of man did not and could not help Pharaoh. And the wisdom of man would not help Joseph either. It was now God's time to act.

JOSEPH COMES BEFORE PHARAOH

The story of Joseph is a story of complete restoration. This anointed dreamer experienced seasons of loss and seasons of favor. But he had learned that God was always with him, not just when life was comfortable and cozy.

It is interesting to note that God cared about Pharaoh as a person, just like he is interested in you. He had sent him dreams to warn him of the coming famine. In fact, both dreams carried the same theme. And Pharaoh woke up with such anxiety that he knew the dreams were significant and supernatural. But when he turned to those who had helped him in the past, they were not able to help him.

Upon overhearing Pharaoh's conversations and lack of interpretation for his dreams, the chief butler remembered Joseph. So he told Pharaoh about the dream interpreter that he met in prison and how he had interpreted his dreams. Pharaoh immediately decided that he should call this Hebrew to help him. With a change of clothes and a fresh shaved face, Joseph was brought out of the prison to appear before him.

God will alert others of our gifting if you will leave the timing with him (Proverbs 22:29). We want to boast or at least get someone else to boast for us. But God must be the one to raise us up in true ministry. For he will never forget us. He knows the best timing for our release.

So Pharaoh hastily sent for Joseph and had him brought into his court. When God's time has come, you will be ready to stand before a king. With a clean-shaven face (free from shame) and a new change of clothes (garments of his righteousness), you, too, will one day stand before the King of kings.

Amazingly, when Joseph found himself before Pharaoh, he did not beg for his release from prison, but with dignity and respect for the mighty Pharaoh, he was quick to acknowledge that only God has the power to interpret dreams. After all, he is the One who gives dreams. Like the Lord Jesus, Joseph would do nothing until the Father revealed it to him (John 5:19, 30). There was a spirit of faith operating in this young man. And he was convinced that God would give him the interpretation.

The life of Joseph gives away God's secrets. It shows us how God prepares, trains, and promotes servants into rulers. The Joseph journey may not be easy for you, but God has not forgotten you or your love for him.

LET'S PRAY

Most High God, I come before you today, thanking you for your kindness and mercy in my life. When I have wandered astray, you have brought me back. When I doubted your ways, you patiently instructed me. Increase my faith in you today. Amen.

16

REVEALING THE
FUTURE—AGAIN

Pharaoh told Joseph, "In my dream I was standing on the bank of the Nile, and up from the river emerged seven healthy, fat cows, and they began to graze in the marshland. Right behind them followed seven other scrawny and emaciated cows. Never have I seen such ugly cows in all the land of Egypt! The seven ugly, scrawny cows ate up the healthy, fat cows, but after consuming them, no one could tell that they had eaten them, for they looked just as bad as before. I awoke with a start, but immediately went back to sleep and had another dream. I saw seven ears of grain, full and ripe, growing on a single stalk. Right behind them sprouted seven thin, shriveled ears, scorched by the east wind. The seven shriveled ears swallowed up the seven healthy ears. I have shared my dreams with my magicians, but no one can give me an interpretation."

GENESIS 41:17–24

Pharaoh's dreams were prophecies of the great famine coming upon Egypt. The Lord gave Pharaoh a seven-year warning that he might prepare for what was coming. God knows the future perfectly. And because of his love for Joseph and his family, God would use these two dreams to not only provide for Egypt but also Israel.

The meaning of the dreams came easy for Joseph because the revealer of mysteries gave him the revelation. For seven years there would be abundance and prosperity. Afterward, there would be seven years of famine. And the dream came to Pharaoh in two forms, which was God's way of confirming and establishing it (two is the number of witness).

Joseph continued, "Let Pharaoh select a very wise and discerning man and set him over the land of Egypt" (Genesis 41:33). Joseph warned Pharaoh and gave him wise counsel. And Pharaoh turned around and gave Joseph the job of preparing and storing away supplies of food. Joseph had no idea that he would be the "very wise and discerning man" that Pharaoh would set over the land. God chose him to be a forerunner, sent before his brothers to save them from the coming famine. Joseph was given the task of overseeing a seven-year agricultural storage project.

Joseph had not only interpreted the dreams, but he had a plan and applied it wisely. If Pharaoh stored up the grain (one-fifth of the harvest in each of the seven bountiful years), then others would have to come and buy their supplies from Egypt. This would make their nation even richer.

The testimony Pharaoh gave of Joseph reveals the godly character of this prophetic dreamer. He said to Joseph, "There is no one as wise and full of insight as you" (41:39). How true this is of Jesus as well. There is simply no one like our heavenly Joseph, our Lord Jesus Christ. He walked in the Spirit without measure. Joseph was a forerunner of our Lord Jesus. His wisdom and understanding for interpreting dreams flowed out of a relationship with God's Spirit. True wisdom comes from the Spirit of Christ (Colossians 2:3).

Joseph was exalted, and Pharaoh honored him above all others. "I hereby place you in charge of all my affairs, and all my people will obey your commands. Only I, the king, will be greater than you!" (Genesis 41:40). In other words, Joseph was made Prime Minister, head of all the people, chief justice, general of the armed forces. Only Pharaoh himself would be over Joseph in all of Egypt. From a prison to the highest office in the land in one day! I believe Joseph was trusted with all of this because it simply did not mean much to him. Joseph had the strange experience of having what other dreamers dream about but not what he dreamed about. Perhaps it was more important to him to have his brothers bow down to him someday because of his dream but all of Egypt? Egypt would finally recognize his gifts but not his brothers. A million people shouting, "Bow the knee" would not do for Joseph as much as eleven brothers doing the same. This exaltation, as glorious as it was, still fell short of what Joseph had been given in his dreams.

So the Lord cleared Joseph's name and his reputation, and Pharaoh affirmed him right on the spot even though he was an accused rapist. Why would anybody trust him?

Have you considered that all you have passed through—the betrayal, the sting of being forgotten, your seemingly endless delay—is all to prepare you for exaltation? The ones God uses the most are often those who have suffered the most. God's name is Redeemer and Savior. He will redeem the years you feel have been lost, and he will save you from the accusations and rejection of those who misunderstand your calling. Just wait and see!

Let's Pray

Lord, even when I don't see that you are working or feel that you're working, I know that, behind the scenes, you are working for my benefit. Life has puzzled me many times, but Lord, you are my confidence and my strength. I love you, Lord! Amen.

17

PROMOTION

"Listen to me, Joseph," Pharaoh continued. "I am placing you in charge of all of Egypt." Then he removed his signet ring, placed it on Joseph's finger, and had him clothed with fine linen robes! He adorned him with a golden collar around his neck. Pharaoh had him ride in the chariot reserved for the second-in-command and sent runners going before him, crying out, "Kneel!" ... Pharaoh also said to Joseph, "I am Pharaoh. No one in all of Egypt will lift a finger without your permission!"

GENESIS 41:41–44

Pharaoh recognized that God was with Joseph, and all of Egypt would now recognize Joseph's authority. What a promotion! Instead of a dingy dungeon, Joseph was free. Instead of prison garments, he received the finest of clothing (the linen garments of a priest!). Joseph lost a robe twice; now he receives a new one.

He who had been dragging fetters of iron was now adorned with a chain of gold. Pharaoh gave Joseph a broad collar made of gold called an usekh. The Egyptians placed these collars on their deities or officials. He was even given the keys to his own chariot, his version of a Rolls Royce.

Joseph is now thirty years old (Genesis 41:46). This is the age at which Jewish men could enter priestly service at the temple and the age at which Jesus began his earthly ministry. Nevertheless, it is an incredibly young age to be awarded the highest governmental position in a powerful nation with the responsibility of running the affairs of the country. This testifies to Joseph's God-given wisdom and grace.

Not only was Joseph a prophet, but he also became an administrator of great wealth. He was given a signet ring, which is like the platinum charge card of his day, signifying the authority of Pharaoh. It fit well with his fine priestly linen garments, the finest clothing any Christian can adorn.

The Lord is about to show favor to a new generation of people like Joseph. They will walk in the authority of a kingly anointing, wearing their priestly garments of purity and displaying the nature of Christ. And they will gather and distribute wealth. Great prosperity will be entrusted to this "Joseph Company." And the nations of the earth will be blessed through the anointing of heaven on their lives.

The church in the nations has been like Joseph with feet in fetters. But the time will come for the church's promotion and for your personal promotion if you partner with the Lord in his kingdom advance. God is sending and raising up both men and women in strategic positions in the world through whom the nations will be changed. They will lead kings in their economic and political affairs. They are the forerunners of an overcoming church that will function in a new wineskin (Matthew 9:7).

THE FIVE-FOLD MINISTRY OF JOSEPH

> Then Joseph was put in charge of everything under the king; he became the master of the palace over all the royal possessions. Pharaoh gave him authority over all the princes of the land, and Joseph became the teacher of wisdom to the king's advisors. (Psalm 105:21–22)

1. Joseph was the overseer of the Egyptian kingdom.

2. Joseph became master of the palace.

3. Joseph became master over all of the royal possessions.

4. Joseph was given authority over all the princes of the land.

5. Joseph became the teacher of wisdom to the king's advisors.

Moses tells us, "Pharaoh gave Joseph a new name: Revealer of Secrets. He also arranged for him to marry the daughter of Potiphera, the priest of Heliopolis. Her name was Asenath. And Joseph took charge over all the land of Egypt" (Genesis 41:45). Pharaoh made Joseph ride in the chariot second to his own. And the people bowed their knees in submission. Pharaoh also gave Joseph a new name, Zaphenath-Paneah, which has been translated from Egyptian with various meanings. The root word for *Zaphenath* is "to hide," and the root word for *Paneah* is "to disclose (explain)." The Greek of the Septuagint can be translated "savior of the world (sustainer of life)." The most common translations are "revealer of secrets," "abundance of life," or "savior of the world." Rabbi Hertz records that the Egyptologists recorded the meaning of the name to be *Tza ph'nat* meaning "bread-man." This is interesting as Christ is referred to as the bread coming out of heaven. He was the true Living Bread. Each of these possible translations points us to Jesus Christ, the true revealer of mysteries, the Savior of the world, and the one God raised from the dead.

Finally, Joseph was also granted the daughter of the priest of On to be his wife. Again, Joseph was a type of Christ who took a bride (church) during the time of the gentiles.

You, my friend, are being groomed for your day of favor and promotion. Remain faithful where you are until God moves you to the place of favor and influence. And just like God did not forget young Joseph, he will not forget you either. Your greatest days are still ahead of you.

LET'S PRAY

Father of Glory, my heart swells with joy when I think of you and your great love for me. You have given me so much and blessed me more than I could ever describe. I know you are with me and will never forsake me. Come close to me today and remind me of your care and favor on my life. I give you my love and praise. Amen.

18

THE PRIME MINISTER
OF EGYPT

*Joseph was thirty years old when he entered the service of Pharaoh,
king of Egypt. Leaving Pharaoh's presence, Joseph traveled
throughout the entire land of Egypt.*

GENESIS 41:46

Thirteen years. That's how long Joseph spent in captivity wondering if his dreams would ever come true. Thirteen long years. But then, it all changed in one day. The prison doors flung open, and Joseph stood before Pharaoh, interpreted his dreams, and then received the title of Prime Minister of all of Egypt. What a difference a day makes!

All this happened when Joseph was only thirty years old. As we already pointed out, thirty is the number of maturity and priestly

70

service. Jesus also began his ministry at thirty, and God visited Ezekiel at thirty. Priests of the old covenant could not begin their priestly duties until they reached thirty (Numbers 4:3). God has a day in store for you. It may be when you are thirty. Or it may be when you are sixty or eighty. It may be the day you cross into your eternal destiny into his palace of love. Yet, you are already being favored, and you may not even realize it. In this day of grace, God has shown us such incredible favor that we have received all spiritual blessings in Christ Jesus on the front end. The Lord places a crown on our head and watches us grow up into it.

And so the seven plenteous years came as Joseph prophesied. During that time, he wisely stored the grain for the future. God's provision during a time of famine was secured by the foresight of his prophet.

> Prior to the famine, Joseph and Asenath, daughter of Potiphera, priest of Heliopolis, had two sons. Joseph named the firstborn Manasseh, saying, "God has made me forget all my troubles and my parental home." The second he named Ephraim, saying, "God has made me fruitful in the land of my suffering." (Genesis 41:50–52)

God was good to Joseph. Prior to the days of famine, blessing was shown in the form of two sons. And he gave his boys names that brought glory to God for his goodness. For his firstborn, *Manasseh* means, "he causes to forget." He named his second son *Ephraim*, which means "twice fruitful." As God exalted Joseph, he forgot his affliction (Job 11:16) and was made fruitful in the land of his affliction. Joseph was quick to humbly acknowledge God in all his ways. "God has made me forget," and "God has made me fruitful."

Mercy always outweighs affliction. The weight of our trials is nothing compared to the weight of the glory that rests on us when we are faithful to God (2 Corinthians 4:17; 1 Peter 4:14). Even in your land of affliction you can become fruitful. In a barren and unlikely soil, God will grow the most pleasant of fruits. Forgetfulness of past burdens leads us into fruitfulness. It takes the mercy of God to cause us to forget our pain.

God's order is Manasseh then Ephraim. God must cause us to forget the prisons of our past before we can become fruitful. Instead of seeking revenge toward our brothers who have harmed us, we must give birth to a "Manasseh." To call your afflictions blessings is to become fruitful and give birth to an "Ephraim." In all these things, we acknowledge that it is the work of God.

The seven years of plenty ended, and the seven years of famine began, "just as Joseph prophesied." The famine was not limited to Egypt but was throughout the region. But in Egypt there was food. And the people in distress cried out to Pharaoh, and by Joseph's prudence, they were spared. The nations of the earth began bowing down before Joseph as they purchased their supplies. And so the wisdom of Joseph brought great wealth into Egypt as the entire world bought food from Pharaoh.

And it was Joseph who held the keys to the vast storehouses of food. Just like Jesus. For in Christ we find the Bread of Life available to us, even when the rest of the world is in a famine. Joseph did not hoard food for himself, but he "opened all the storehouses" (Genesis 41:56). He was an excellent administrator, a wise manager of Egypt's resources. The Lord had promoted him because he had passed the test of the pit and the prison and grew in character. So when the Lord saw that he was ready, the Lord promoted him to great power. And he handled it all without pride or arrogance.

Joseph was a man who was prepared to rule with wisdom, and he would use his position of authority to provide for others.

God now had a man that he could use as a deliverer. But Joseph did not take advantage of his situation to quickly run off to rescue his family. He knew that God was in control and that he'd been raised up by God to wear a special yoke—the yoke of serving the will of God and nothing else. It took a famine to restore and reconcile Joseph's family. And Father God will use the difficulties of our lives to bring the churches back together again in sweet unity. Do not underestimate what God might be doing behind the scenes. He can turn it all around. The enemy will not have the last say.

There is a Joseph company of believers who have submitted their lives to the furnace of affliction where the Word of God will be purified in their earthen vessel seven times (Psalm 12:6). They will become a storehouse of plenty for those in famine. They may be locked up and sealed in the King's prison for now, but the doors of favor will open, and they will be released to give out bread to the hungry nations of the earth.

LET'S PRAY

Lord, I love your presence. As I look back upon the seasons of my life, I find your fingerprints everywhere. The beauty of your fellowship sustains me. Faithfully you draw me, day after day, into the garden of your love. Keep bringing me closer and closer to you, Lord, I pray. Amen.

19

JOSEPH'S DREAM FULFILLED

One day, Joseph's ten brothers came and bowed down before him
with their faces on the ground.

GENESIS 42:6

The good thing about the famine was that it sent Joseph's brothers out looking for food and eventually to him. There was no other place where they could go. There was just no other option except death by starvation. Abraham, Isaac, and each of Joseph's brothers met with famine in Canaan. This was a test to their faith, so much so that they begin to look for a better land, a heavenly one (Hebrews 11:14–16).

Joseph's ten brothers set out for Egypt on a journey of eight to ten days to buy food for their exceptionally large families (Genesis 46:26). So Jacob said good-bye to ten of his sons while Benjamin remained with him in Canaan. And upon their arrival in Egypt, the ten brothers were ushered into the presence of the Prime Minister. They must have been somewhat uncomfortable before this powerful man. They were simple shepherds with no clue that the Prime Minister was their brother Joseph, clothed in royal robes of honor and the headdress of Egypt. Joseph's dream had come true as his brothers bowed down before him.

What would he say to them after all these years? Who knows, maybe he had been waiting for them all along. He was seventeen when he had his dreams. And at the age of thirty, he was exalted over Egypt. Nine years later, at the age of thirty-nine, here he is, and his brothers are buying grain from him. He had to wait twenty-two years for the fulfillment of his dreams. Now here they were bowing down before him. What a feeling that must have been!

When they came before him, Joseph knew who they were, even though they did not recognize him. It was just as he had dreamed it…almost. He remembered their sheaves of wheat bowing down before him. But what about the eleven stars bowing down? There were only ten of them. Where was the eleventh?

Why didn't Joseph immediately reveal himself to his brothers? Why did he pretend that he believed they were spies? From a human standpoint you would think that Joseph would have been happy for an instant reconciliation with them. But Joseph was a broken man and was prepared to deliver others.

Joseph spoke and related with them in such a way that their hearts would be revealed and exposed. Did Joseph wonder if they had done to Benjamin what they had done to him? It was not a spirit of revenge driving Joseph but a true love for his brothers and for the ways of God. The tests Joseph took them through were designed by God to bring them to repentance. Joseph "pretended he didn't know them and spoke to them harshly" (42:7).

After Joseph accused them of being spies, their reply was, "No, master, we've come to buy food. We, your servants, are honest men; we'd never think of spying! We're blood brothers, sons of one man" (v. 10). They were all related to each other—even to the one brother they betrayed and sold into slavery. As Joseph continued to question them, they even acknowledged that one of them was "no more" (v. 13). His interrogation forced them to refer to the sin they had covered up, and the one who was no more was standing before them as ruler and prince.

Since they protested and said that they were honest men, Joseph gave them a chance to prove it and said, "Unless your younger brother comes here and presents himself here before me, then as surely as Pharaoh lives, you shall not depart from here!" (v. 15). Four times Joseph accused them of being in Egypt under the pretense of spying on the land (vv. 9, 12, 14, 16). And he puts them in confinement for three days, perhaps to let them know what it felt like to be in prison for all those many years, not to punish them but to prepare them. All they could do was conclude that God had done this because of what they had done to Joseph.

Guilt troubles the soul and keeps you from the sweet discovery of mercy and forgiveness. The brother's guilt would soon be washed away but not until Joseph tested their sincerity.

LET'S PRAY

Lord, I praise you for taking away the guilt and shame of sin. Anoint me with the oil of your Holy Spirit. Let it saturate me until every cell in my body is dripping with the fragrance of your love. Transform me from the inside out. I want to smell like you and look like you, leaving the impact of your glory everywhere I go today. Amen.

20

SIMEON, THE HOSTAGE

*With Joseph standing there, they began to speak among themselves,
saying, "Look what's happened to us! We're being punished for
what we did to Joseph long ago. We heard his cries of anguish and
saw the agony of his soul when he begged us for mercy, but we
turned a deaf ear. That's why all this trouble has come upon us!"
Then Reuben spoke up, "Didn't I tell you not to sin against the
boy? But you wouldn't listen! So now we're paying the price for his
murder!" They had no clue that Joseph understood every word, for
he had been speaking to them through an interpreter.*

GENESIS 42:21–23

On the third day, Joseph released all but Simeon, who remained
as a hostage. He released the other ten brothers to return to Jacob
and to go for Benjamin, whom Joseph wanted to see. And as they
prepared to leave, they began to discuss the situation among

themselves in their own Hebrew language, not realizing that the brother they had betrayed understood their every word.

Their guilt had finally surfaced. Time does not wear out the guilt of sin. Their consciences were originally asleep, but God has once again awakened them. Reuben was convinced that their difficulties in Egypt are the result of bloodguilt. They could no longer blame the favoritism of Jacob or excuse their sin. They began to realize the suffering that they had inflicted upon their little brother, Joseph, as he had cried out for their help. And they remembered the look in his eyes as they sold him into slavery.

Two decades could not remove the stain of their guilty consciences. As they stood there discussing these things, Joseph understood every word they said, and he couldn't take it any longer. He had to turn away to weep in private. "Deeply affected by what he heard, Joseph began to weep and hurriedly left their presence. After he had composed himself, he returned to them, and pointing to Simeon, said, 'This one will remain here'" (42:24). What secret love Joseph had for his brothers. Every time he called the name of his son, Manasseh, he thought, *God has made me forget all my troubles and my parental home.* Joseph was in tune with the timing of God and knew that it was not yet the time to reveal himself. But before he left them, he showed them a token of mercy.

As the nine brothers left for Canaan, Joseph gave them sacks of grain for their journey. And at his orders, Joseph's steward placed the brother's money back in their sacks of grain. In other words, Joseph paid for the grain himself. He loved his brothers and because of his secret love for them, he paid their debt (Isaiah 55:1). They did not deserve the grain, and they didn't deserve to get their money back, but mercy prevailed. Placing their money back in their sacks was a part of Joseph's wise plan to test his brothers.[8]

Along the way home, one of the brothers opened his sack of grain to feed his donkey and found the silver. And "He shouted to his brothers, 'My money! Look, someone put my money back in my sack!' Troubled and trembling, they said to each other, 'What in the world has God done to us?'" (Genesis 42:28–29). Their unconfessed sin brought fear to their hearts. And so they concluded that God was the author of these strange events. When the Lord activates your conscience, you see things from a new perspective. They could see God in their situation. And they were trembling because they were getting closer and closer to their worst fear. They were afraid that their father would find out what they had done to Joseph.

"Their father Jacob said to his sons, 'You have taken away my children! First, Joseph is gone, and now Simeon! And now, you want to take Benjamin from me! Everything is against me!'" (Genesis 42:36). Have you ever said words like these: "Everything is against me"? When we say that, we are not realizing that, on the contrary, everything is working for our good (Romans 8:28). And Jacob had no clue either. He did not realize that it was all going to work out for him and his loved ones. What we interpret as our worst days, God calls his handiwork. He is creating us into the image of Jesus, and he knows that we will not change without being shaken loose from our comfort zone. When it looks like everything is against you, do not forget that, "If God has determined to stand with us, tell me, who then could ever stand against us?" (v. 31).

LET'S PRAY

Lord, your words are like liquid love pouring over me. Your promises are the comfort of my soul. They flood my senses and awaken my heart. I drink them in until I am overflowing with grace and truth. They have become a part of me, dwelling within my frailty. Let me drink constantly of the reality of your love today. I'm ruined for anything else. Amen.

21

BENJAMIN

Reuben said, "Father, you may put my two sons to death if I fail to bring Benjamin back to you! Trust me—I will bring him back!" But Jacob replied, "I can't let my son Benjamin go with you. For his brother is dead, and of Rachel's sons, he alone is left. If he were to meet with disaster on your journey, I would die of grief! You will send my white hair and broken heart sorrowing down to the grave!"

GENESIS 42:37–38

Due to the severity of the famine, Jacob changes his mind and has no other choice than to send his sons back to Egypt. (Father God knows how to use our places of "famine" to force us into the place of true nourishment.) At this point, Judah reminds his father that if they fail to take Benjamin along that they will not be able to purchase the food. And without Benjamin, they would not have the boldness to approach the Egyptian ruler again. Little did they know that Joseph had primarily devised this plan so that he might finally be able to see his youngest brother.

So Judah decides to offer his very life as a guarantee that Benjamin would return back home safely with them. What a change of heart this was for Judah! Perhaps his experience with Tamar had led him to repentance (Genesis 38). This is a picture of the One who would come as a son of Judah, a lion from the tribe of Judah, to offer his life as a ransom for many, our Lord Jesus Christ.

Benjamin's name means "son of my right hand." Jacob's sons told him, essentially, "You won't see Joseph's face until he sees Benjamin." This applies to the One greater than Joseph. Until he has sons of his right hand, an overcoming company of sons and daughters who sit and reign with him in victory (Revelation 3:21), our heavenly Joseph will be kept from us. When the church matures into the full measure of sonship, we will see him whom our soul loves.

Before they left, Jacob instructed his sons to take gifts to this strange ruler of Egypt and to double the amount of silver that was placed in their grain sacks. Perhaps these gifts would soften the heart of this harsh man: "Take some balm and some honey, spices and myrrh, pistachio nuts and almonds" (Genesis 43:11). This was Jacob's scheme, as though the life of Judah was not enough of a guarantee. These token gifts were the best products of the land. Jacob was attempting to gain favor, rather than placing his trust in God. It had worked years before with Esau, perhaps it would work now. So Jacob blessed his sons in the name of El Shaddai and off they went.

Can you imagine what the brothers were thinking as they traveled to Egypt? Ten scared men on a trip to buy food and deliver their brother, Simeon. They were not rejoicing but deeply concerned about what would happen. Would the ruler take Benjamin hostage also? Would he ask about the silver that was in the mouth of their sacks? What a trial this was for Jacob! God was emptying his life again, as though taking everything that was precious from him.

After Benjamin left with his brothers, Jacob was all alone. Rachel was dead and buried, Joseph had been killed, the strange Prime Minister of Egypt was holding Simeon hostage, and now beloved Benjamin had been taken from him too. Jacob had nothing left of those he loved. Night after night, Jacob realized that God was emptying him once again. And the more Jacob waited, the more he suffered. And the more he suffered, the more he matured.

JOSEPH RECEIVES HIS ELEVEN BROTHERS

Finally, the brothers arrive in Egypt to purchase more food. They come returning the silver they discovered in the mouth of their sacks of grain. And they are returning with Benjamin, hoping Simeon would be freed. They have no idea what awaits them in Egypt as they come to stand before this strange ruler, Joseph. They didn't know that the rejected brother, the brother that they had sold into slavery, had actually been sent ahead of them into Egypt to deliver them. As they brought their gifts, they had no clue that this strange ruler is about to feast with them.

When Joseph saw Benjamin, his little brother, he felt moved in tenderness toward his other brothers. He instructed his chief steward to kill an animal and to prepare a feast in his own house. And the brothers felt paralyzed with fear, and though they presumed the worst, Joseph was filled with mercy and planned the best for them. Isn't that the way? We assume that God, our Father, is ready to punish us when we goof up, but actually, he is ready to rescue us and has prepared a feast for our homecoming.

LET'S PRAY

Father, your love for me is amazing. You are patient with me, tolerate my weakness, and forgive me continually. I love everything about you, my Father. Thank you for a love that changes me from the inside out. Today, I give myself to you, to be loved by you and to give your love away to others. In Jesus' name. Amen.

22

BROTHERS WELCOME

*When Joseph saw his brother Benjamin with them, he said to his
chief servant, "Bring the men to my house and make them feel at
home. Butcher an animal and prepare a meal, for these men are to
dine with me at noon." Joseph's chief servant did as he was told and
brought the men to Joseph's house.*

GENESIS 43:16–17

Joseph's brothers must have been wondering why the Prime
Minister of Egypt would invite them, a dusty foreign tribe of
Hebrew nomads, to feast with him. Why would he treat them
with such unusual dignity? They thought that he might want to
get even with them, but they never expected him to invite them to
a feast. That never even crossed their minds. Fear always brings us
to a false conclusion.

Joseph's steward washed their feet and gave fodder to their

donkeys. Treated with respect, these eleven brothers had their feet washed by Egyptian servants while they had fully expected a severe punishment. The grace of God is so surprising and amazing. And then they bowed before Joseph once more. This time it was all his brothers, all eleven of them, fulfilling Joseph's dream. One by one they came before Joseph, bowed down to him, and presented him their gifts. How deeply moving this must have been to Joseph!

> The men laid out their gifts to present to Joseph, for they were told he would appear before them at noon and would dine with them. When Joseph came home, they presented to him the gifts they had brought with them into the house. They each bowed low before him with their faces to the ground. He asked them how the family was doing, saying, "You mentioned your aging father; is he still alive? Is he doing well?" (43:25–27)

Then came an emotionally charged moment when Joseph lifted his eyes and saw his own mother's son, Benjamin. And his eyes began to fill with tears as he saw him face-to-face. This was his full blood brother.

"Joseph hastily left the room, for he was overwhelmed with feelings of love for his brother and on the verge of tears. He went into a private room and sobbed, as tears ran down his cheeks" (v. 30). All at once, this world leader, the captain over millions, collapsed inside. Now it was all finally beginning to make sense—all the loneliness, those dark days in prison, the misunderstanding, and the pain of rejection. A family shattered for over two decades was being reunited.

It took great discipline for Joseph to keep his secret from them.

For Joseph's heart had been moved in tenderness and affection for his long-lost family. Feelings he had from his boyhood surfaced again in his heart and like a little boy, he missed his daddy.

When his weeping finally subsided, he gained his composure and sat down to dinner to eat with them. And he sat them in their birth order and spread the tables with a feast fit for a prince. Finally, he had his family feasting together again, but there was still a wall between them.

> Now, the brothers had been seated before Joseph in their
> birth order, from the firstborn at one end of the table
> to the youngest at the other end. They were all stunned
> when they realized the seating arrangement and looked
> at each other in astonishment. (v. 33)

As they noticed the order of seating, the brothers were amazed but still had no clue. There are nearly 39,917,000 different orders in which eleven individuals could be seated. What must they have been thinking? Did they believe he had supernatural wisdom so that he knew their birth order?

"Eleven plates of food were taken from Joseph's table and set in front of each of them, but Benjamin's portion was five times more than any of theirs! They feasted and drank their fill with Joseph until they all became drunk" (v. 34). What a feast was before them! They had not eaten like this for months, maybe even years. And because of their cultural distinctions, Joseph seated the Egyptians at one table, his brothers at a different table, and himself at another. He was being sensitive to the culture and their beliefs of not eating with gentiles. Before the day was over, they were comfortable with one another, and he had convinced them that he was truly a friend. It is the same with our Lord Jesus. When we feast at his table, we begin to drop our guard and realize that he truly is our friend.

THE TEST OF JEALOUSY

Joseph let them understand that Benjamin was his favorite, for he had him served five portions more of food then all the others. Five times more meat, five times more vegetables, five servings of cakes and pies—five times more of everything! Why would Joseph give more to Benjamin? Was he merely following the steps of his father's favoritism that brought all of this on? No.

Joseph was testing his brothers to see if they would be jealous again. Were they truly broken? Could they endure seeing one brother favored over all the others and still rejoice? Would they get rid of Benjamin like they had him? What if one of your friends received five times as much of gifts, talents, and anointing as you? This was the test Joseph presented to them.

You would surmise that Joseph's brothers would figure out who was before them. But he appeared to them as an Egyptian by his behavior and dress. Surely, they could see some resemblance with this man and their brother. Didn't they recognize his voice, even though he spoke in another language? Didn't they notice how he broke down when he spoke with Benjamin? How else would he have known their birth order? Hadn't they bowed down to him just like Joseph had said they would?

Why didn't they realize who he was? The same way we fail to realize that Jesus is the One who deals with us and cares for us and speaks with us and walks with us. We do not recognize our Beloved, just as they did not recognize Joseph.

LET'S PRAY

Lord, your grace surprises me. When I deserve a lecture, you give me a kiss. When I feel most unworthy, you lift up my head again and remove my shame. I am undone when I think of your grace and how much you love me! Help me today to walk in the light of your love in all that I do. Amen.

23

JOSEPH'S SILVER GOBLET

*Joseph ordered his chief servant, "Fill the men's sacks with grain,
with as much as they can hold, and put each one's money back in
the mouth of his bag. As for the youngest one, place my silver goblet
in the mouth of his sack, along with the money he paid for his
grain." And he did as Joseph said. At dawn, the men loaded their
donkeys and set off for home.*

GENESIS 44:1–3

As the eleven brothers left Egypt for Canaan, they had every
reason for joy. They had not been arrested or killed for stealing
the silver to pay for the grain. Simeon had been safely released,
and Benjamin was traveling safely back with them to their father.
They even had full sacks of grain to feed their hungry families.
And they had just been honored guests at the house of this world
leader, Joseph…it was a good day.

But there is one last test that Joseph presents his brothers as they leave for home. As a wise leader Joseph wanted nothing more than to reveal his true identity to his brothers, but first, they must show signs of deep maturity and lasting repentance. He wanted to see in his brothers some of the same attitude God had cultivated in him. Their unknown antagonist was actually their best friend. He was God's vessel to preserve their life and prepare them for greatness. So here is their final exam.

Joseph ordered his chief servant, "Fill the men's sacks with grain, with as much as they can hold, and put each one's money back in the mouth of his bag. As for the youngest one, place my silver goblet in the mouth of his sack, along with the money he paid for his grain."

Just think about this, the first time the ten brothers came to Egypt, Joseph imprisoned Simeon and had their silver placed back into their nine sacks of grain. The second time, they returned with Benjamin, and Joseph had all their silver placed back into their eleven sacks. The total number of the portions of silver returned was twenty—the very same amount of silver that was paid for Joseph (37:28).

At daybreak the next day, they all left. And then a short time later Joseph sent his steward to catch up with them and tell them how wicked they were for stealing his silver cup! They were dumb-founded. How could this be? They were sure that none of them had done anything wrong.

"If any of your servants is found to have it, then he will die, and the rest of us will become your master's slaves!" "Very well then," Joseph's servant replied, "as you have said. But I will show you leniency. The one who has it will be my slave, but the rest of you will go free." Each one quickly lowered his bag to the ground and opened it. Then the chief servant searched each bag, beginning with the oldest and ending with the youngest—and he found the silver goblet in Benjamin's bag! Aghast, the brothers ripped their clothes in despair. They all loaded their donkeys again and returned to the city. (44:9–13)

While the servant was opening and closing the sacks, they stood by quite satisfied that they had done nothing. They even agreed that if one of them were found to have taken the cup, he would become a slave for life. Starting with the oldest on down to the youngest, they looked into all the sacks until they came to Benjamin's…And they found Joseph's silver goblet in Benjamin's sack.

Can you imagine what they were feeling? They had been framed! Why would Joseph want to hide their money back in their sacks again? Did he just want to hurt them? Why would he instruct his steward to place his own silver goblet inside Benjamin's grain sack? What was up? Was God behind this?

Joseph was testing their loyalty. Would they stand with Benjamin and love him, or would they sacrifice Benjamin like they had done to him? Would they be loyal brothers now? Joseph was giving them a chance to turn away from his younger brother as they had with him. For as Joseph dined with them the day before, he could tell that they were suffering with guilt. He wanted to show them they could be totally free now.

The Lord is good at exposing us and uncovering our secrets. The silver cup was a ploy. The brothers were innocent, but they had done things far worse and thought they'd gotten away with it. They hadn't stolen Joseph's silver cup, but they had stolen Joseph's dignity when they threw him into a pit and sold him as a slave. They were responsible for all of Joseph's afflictions. And this was

God's way of revealing their hearts through this false accusation that they had to endure. And Judah was the first to acknowledge their guilt toward Joseph.

For the third time, Joseph's brothers bowed before him. What a sight it was for Joseph's heart to see them all return. He was testing them because he wanted to know if they had really changed. The fact that they stood with Benjamin proved their loyalty as brothers. And Judah's confession was amazing, "What can we say, my lord? How can we plead our case? How can we prove our innocence? God has revealed the guilt of your servants" (44:16). They passed the test with a resounding *A*.

Joseph was truly doing them a kindness. He was giving them a chance to pass a test they had once failed. They could free themselves of their guilt, not just by the mercy of Joseph but also by the fruits of repentance. It was very likely that these brothers were going to have a hard time forgiving themselves for what they had done. Have you ever had that problem? *If only I had...* or *I should have...* The kindest thing that could happen to each of us after committing a horrible sin would be to discover that we have no desire to do it again. Guilt and fear are gone. And our freedom soars again.

The way that Joseph dealt with his brothers is the way that Jesus deals with us. And he doesn't test us so that we'll fail, but he does it to prove that we've changed, and now we can forgive ourselves.

LET'S PRAY

Father, your ways are past finding out. Your mysteries fascinate me. I love the ways you bring me out of messes into miracles. Keep dealing with my heart to purify and make me holy. And give me grace to continue my journey with my faith strong and my heart tender. Amen.

24

PLEADING FOR BENJAMIN

*Judah continued, "My lord, if I went to your servant, my father,
without [Benjamin], and he saw that the boy was not with us, he
would die! His very life is wrapped up with the life of the boy. Now
he is so old that the grief of his loss would kill him. Furthermore, I,
your servant, have guaranteed the boy's safety to my father. I told
him, 'If I don't return the boy back to you, I will bear the blame
before you, my father, for the rest of my life!' So, please let me take
the place of the boy, and I will remain here as a slave to you, my
lord. Please let the boy go back with his brothers. How could I
return to my father without the boy? I don't want to witness the
woe and grief that would overtake my father."*

GENESIS 44:30–34

As Judah spoke for his brothers, he didn't attempt to justify himself or pass the blame off onto Benjamin, unlike what he tried to do in the past. Judah acknowledges that the guilt of their past was now discovered and that God had done this, for the Lord was dealing with them for their hidden sin. Now they stand vulnerable before their disguised brother Joseph, helpless and at the mercy of their rejected sibling. And so Joseph sentences them with an air of justice. They were to leave Benjamin behind, for only he was the one who was proven guilty—the others could leave freely. Joseph was giving them another chance to turn their backs again on a brother.

But Judah draws near and begins to plead for the life of Benjamin. Judah begs Joseph to take his life in place of his little brother. He became his younger brother's mediator as he begged to be Benjamin's substitute. And then he begins to review their family history, as though Joseph didn't know it. He was hoping that then maybe Joseph would have mercy as he made a claim for the release of Benjamin.

Judah had no idea how his words triggered a deep emotional place in Joseph's heart. He touched on memories that were near and dear to Joseph's heart, touching on some of his most tender feelings. And so Judah went on to explain their love for their father, Jacob, and how important the life of Benjamin was to him, having lost Joseph already. Judah uses the word *father* thirteen times in his speech, without one clue of how deeply this touched Joseph each time he mentioned his father.

Few scenes in the Scripture come close to the power and emotion of this moment. Without his knowledge, Judah presses on with great sincerity, "My Lord, if I went to your servant, my father, without the boy and if he sees that the boy was not with us, he would die! His very life is wrapped up with the life of the boy. Now he is so old that the grief of his loss would kill him." Love is flowing from Judah.

He loves his father, and he loves his brother Benjamin. What a change has taken place in Judah's heart! And he acknowledges the deep attachment of Jacob to Benjamin. He continues, "Furthermore, I, your servant, have guaranteed the boy's safety to my father. I told him, 'If I don't return the boy back to you, I will bear the blame before you, my father, for the rest of my life!'" Jacob and Benjamin were bound together in the bundle of life. Judah could not allow his father to go through another separation from the loss of a beloved son. And he finally realized the pain he had caused his father in betraying Joseph and didn't want to repeat his sin with Benjamin. So he offers himself in the place of his brother.

"So, please let me take the place of the boy, and I will remain here as a slave to you, my lord. Please let the boy go back with his brothers." What humility he shows as he considers Benjamin better than himself—what self-sacrificial loyalty. These words are coming from the very one who, twenty-two years earlier, said along with his brothers, "Here comes this dream expert. Let's kill him and throw his body into one of these dry wells. We can say a wild animal ate him." Now he's pleading for Benjamin.

Judah is now a true intercessor, a transformed man. This is where God wants to take all of his people. The healing of the breach. It doesn't happen only through repentance but also through sacrificial love, showing that we will lay down our lives for our brothers. There is no greater love than this. But there is One whose love is even more than a brother. The faithful Lion of Judah deserves eternal praise. He's the One who offered himself as a sacrifice for sin; he's the One who died for all. And he was a descendent of Judah (Hebrews 7:14). Like his father Judah, he not only made intercession for the transgressors, but he also became their substitute, the innocent for the guilty, bearing the sin of the world. So now the Father doesn't look at our shame but gazes on his beloved Son.

LET'S PRAY

Father, you are so wise and so loving. You know exactly what I need in order to love you more. Help me to see your hand at work in my life today. Knowing that you never let go of me and that you never make a mistake. Open my eyes, Lord, to see you working in me to make me more like your Son. Amen.

25

JOSEPH REVEALED

Joseph could no longer contain his pent-up feelings, so he cried out to his attendants, "Leave the room!" So no one was there when Joseph revealed his identity to his brothers. He began to weep so loudly that the Egyptians heard it—even as far away as Pharaoh's house! Joseph, through his tears, said to his brothers in Hebrew: "I am Joseph! Is father still alive?" His brothers stood there stunned, scared, and speechless.

GENESIS 45:1–3

The family secret was a secret no more! Holding this secret from his brothers for nearly a year, Joseph could not contain himself any longer. He must reveal himself to those he loved. So he ordered all the Egyptians and the interpreter to leave. And as Joseph waited for the last Egyptian to file out of the room the tears erupted. His buried emotions rose up within him, and he could contain it no more. "He began to weep so loudly that the Egyptians heard him—even as far as Pharaoh's house!" Tears were streaming down his face.

His simple statement, "I am Joseph!" must have sounded like a thunderbolt in their ears. Can you just imagine how much this confession blew them away? Confused thoughts must have suddenly begun to tumble around in their minds. What did he just say? How could this strange ruler in Egypt know the name of their deceased brother? Surely he wasn't their brother? In stunned silence they backed away. They were speechless.

> Joseph said to his brothers, "Please, come close to me."
> Inching forward, they came close to him. Then Joseph
> said, "It's me—your brother—whom you sold into slavery
> in Egypt. I am Joseph! Now don't be grieved. Don't
> blame yourselves because you sold me here. It was God
> who sent me ahead of you in order to save lives…God
> sent me ahead of you to ensure that you would live and
> have descendants. He has saved your lives through this
> marvelous act of deliverance. So, it was God, not you,
> who sent me here." (vv. 4–5, 7–8)

"PLEASE, COME CLOSE TO ME"

Joseph saw in their eyes their fear and bewilderment. Instead of saying, "Get out of here! You betrayed me!" he said, "Please, come close to me." Many are those who would have pushed away and made them pay the price for their sin, but Joseph began to encourage the very ones who hurt him the most.

Joseph's compassion for his brothers ran deep. For the third time he told them that it was God, not they, who orchestrated all the events to bring him to the throne. Once painfully betrayed by them, Joseph now began to encourage the brothers. Yes, this was their long-lost brother, and they were hearing kind words from a loving, forgiving heart. And as the words washed over them, his grace and kindness overruled their feelings of guilt. Through his tears he convinced them not to dwell on their sins but on how God was working through it all. Joseph had been sent by God ahead of them to preserve their lives. Without even realizing it, Joseph's brothers were helping the Lord fulfill his promise to Abraham (Genesis 12:1–3; Psalm 105:17).

Today, we must learn to see that even those who hurt us the most may be those who move us toward the throne. If you see yourself in the hands of a loving God, not in the hands of others, you will not be offended. If Joseph's brothers had not sold him into slavery, how would his dreams have been fulfilled? Some of your dreams will never come true until you can handle both mistreatment and betrayal with forgiving love (Mark 11:25; Luke 23:34).

There is not another person who could have been offended to the degree that Joseph could have been at his brothers, yet he didn't even have the slightest desire for revenge. He not only forgave them, but he also comforted them and received them in love. His hurt and pain were redemptive. And Joseph never could have brought his brothers to repentance if he had been nursing a grudge. The king's prison had taken all of that out of him.

What a scene. The one betrayed, offended, and sold into slavery now comforts those who abused him. God had worked a deep work in Joseph's life. Often, when Christians forgive someone, they say, "Yes, I forgive you, but you really need to know the seriousness of what you did to me." This kind of forgiveness is not true forgiveness. It's making others your debtors. But Joseph comforted his offenders and told them, "Now don't be grieved. Don't blame yourselves." Joseph regarded his brothers as God's helpers, our sweet crucifiers. I thank the Lord for his helpers that he uses to teach me, for they help to bring forth Christ's love in me in a far deeper way. They disciple us.

God did not cause the problem, but the enemy did. God used it and turned it all around for good. No matter what we face, we are still in the Lord's hands; we're not in the hands of others, and we don't need to be offended. Your offenses, those areas where you stumble over the words and deeds of your brothers, are actually prophecies of the next area God is going to break through for you. The more you're offended, wounded, and mistreated, the more good will come. We must always have our eyes on the God who overcomes evil with virtue.

LET'S PRAY

Father, you are perfect in all of your ways. Your grace and mercy are astounding to me. You have forgiven me all my sins. I could never repay you for all the gifts and love you have showered upon my life. Yet, I want to live my life in a way that pleases your heart. Help me do just that today, in Jesus' name. Amen.

26

A MODEL OF FORGIVENESS

"The famine has now endured for two years, and the land will not bear fruit for five more years. God sent me ahead of you to ensure that you would live and have descendants. He has saved your lives through this marvelous act of deliverance. So it was God, not you, who sent me here. God has made me a father to Pharaoh, the master of his entire household, and the ruler over all of Egypt."

GENESIS 45:6–8

God is interested in making your dreams come true, but he longs even more to bring forth Christ within you (Galatians 4:19). Joseph's dreams were fulfilled by those who offended him. They were the ones that brought him to the throne.

To be unwilling to forgive your betrayers is to be shortsighted. Nevertheless, if you could only see into God's purpose, you would never seek revenge. For Joseph, the good that came was not just for him, but it was for his whole family also. Not just to save a kingdom in Egypt but to preserve a remnant of Israelites.

When we have vision, we understand that much of what we must experience is for the benefit of others as much as it is for us. Whatever happens to you will work for your good and for the good of the kingdom of God. Is this your mindset today? Perhaps you've wanted to be a great leader like Joseph. It may be that the Lord will answer this prayer by allowing you to go through the suffering and betrayal that Joseph faced beforehand. And you may also be tested in the area of forgiving those who offend you, like he did first.

Joseph suffered constantly from the age of seventeen until he was thirty. All of these sufferings produced great character and leadership traits in this dreamer. Someday you will be released from your suffering as he was. As you are patient and deny yourself and as you posture your heart to forgive all who have wounded you, a deliverer's anointing will come upon you as well.

Imagine if you could have told Joseph's brothers ahead of time what was to come: (1) They would find Joseph alive, (2) Joseph would totally forgive their sin, and (3) God was behind everything that had happened to them. They couldn't have imagined this even in their wildest dreams. Yet this is like your salvation: (1) Jesus is alive! (2) He has forgiven you all your sins. (3) Your life is his handiwork, his poetry (Ephesians 2:10).

Notice the model Joseph gives us of forgiveness:

1. Total forgiveness is not wanting others to know how we have been hurt. Joseph insisted that the Egyptians leave the room. He didn't want them to know how his brothers had hurt him. It's an unforgiving spirit that wants to tell others how we've been offended. With

Joseph, it was going to be a secret buried forever. This is true forgiveness.

2. Total forgiveness will put others at ease, relieving their guilt. His brothers were deeply troubled in his presence—how would Joseph treat them now? Hatred hopes that others feel uneasy and relive their guilt. We want to make them squirm. Joseph told them to "come close to me." He sought to ease their pain and sorrow. This is true forgiveness.

3. Total forgiveness makes it easy for others to forgive themselves. Joseph explained that God has overruled and brought him to the throne to preserve their lives. He pointed them to God as the sovereign and wise God. Joseph told them, "It wasn't you...it was God." Joseph restored to his offenders a sense of dignity. This is true forgiveness.

4. Total forgiveness is having a heart that is ready to restore a former relationship. Joseph not only forgave his brothers, but he also longed to live with them again. So he instructed them to return to Canaan and to bring their father and all of their possessions back with them. He wanted the full restoration of their relationship as a family. This is true forgiveness.

Joseph also had a divine perspective. As he told his family: "So, it was God, not you, who sent me here. God has made me a father to Pharaoh, master to his entire household, and the ruler over all of Egypt."

God has a plan for you, and his plan will come to pass. Joseph was a man who continually walked with divine perspective. Just like Joseph we, too, must always see that God is the great guide of our lives. He will use our suffering as preparation and our disappointment as training just like he did with Joseph to prepare him to be a father to Pharaoh. Your life is taking you into the place of becoming a blessing to the lost and to your brothers. Hang in there, young Joseph.

Let's Pray

Father, I thank you for the example of Joseph's life. The way he forgave those who hurt him the most stirs my soul. I want that forgiveness to flow through my life. Enable me, by your grace, to love and forgive the way Joseph did…the way you have forgiven me. I love you, Father. Amen.

27

THE DELIVERER

*[Joseph said to his brothers:] "Hurry back to my father and tell him
that you have found me alive. Tell him, 'This is what your son Joseph
says, "God has made me ruler of all Egypt. Come to me without
delay. You will settle in the land of Goshen,⁹ where you will be near
me—you and all your children and your grandchildren, your flocks
and herds and all that you possess. For there will be five more years
of famine, but I will provide all that you need to live in Goshen. You,
your household, and all that you have will not live in poverty.""'*

GENESIS 45:9–11

Joseph not only forgave them; he also makes them an offer
they cannot refuse. He invites his brothers to move their family
to Egypt in order to survive the famine. He wants it made clear
to Jacob that it was God who elevated Joseph over all the land of
Egypt. For their family's destiny to be fulfilled, they had to come

107

and dwell in Egypt. However, for the brothers to tell Jacob that Joseph was alive meant they would have to tell him how they betrayed him and sold him to Egypt. This open confession would be necessary to heal the family of their wounds. Truly, Father knows best.

All that transpired that amazing day was a prophetic portrayal of the glorious reconciliation that will one day occur between Yeshua and his alienated Jewish brothers. Through the last two thousand years, he has been unrecognizable to the Jewish people in his "gentile" garb, as it were, and in his identity as a Christian conqueror. But the time will come when hearts will soften in repentance towards the Father, that Yeshua will reveal his full identity as their Jewish brother and Messiah. The past will be redeemed, and new life and true shalom will burst forth like a fountain, and the whole house of David will move fully from exile to redemption.

JOSEPH KISSES HIS BETRAYERS

> "Then Joseph threw his arms around Benjamin's neck, sobbing, and Benjamin wept on Joseph's neck. With tears streaming down his face, Joseph kissed each brother, one by one. After their tearful, emotional embrace, they took time to speak brother-to-brother." (vv. 14–15)

The kiss of Judah was the kiss of betrayal, but here we find Joseph kissing those who betrayed him. Beginning with Benjamin, his youngest brother, Joseph kissed them and restored his fellowship with them all. Benjamin was only a year old when Joseph was separated from them. As Joseph and Benjamin wept together, they both likely remembered their mother Rachel, who died giving birth to Benjamin.

Joseph embraced each one and blessed them all and spoke freely with them. How sweet is restored communion with our brothers!

Imagine how all this touched Pharaoh when he heard about their reunion. He was told about the strong weeping that rang through Joseph's house and the puzzling way Joseph had dealt with them and finally revealed himself to his brothers. Pharaoh realized that something strange was taking place, and it pleased him to see Joseph's true character. Our attitude reveals true greatness.

> The news reached Pharaoh's house: "Joseph's brothers have come." Pharaoh and his officials were greatly pleased when they heard it. Pharaoh said to Joseph, "Tell your brothers: 'Load your donkeys and return to Canaan. Get your father and your families and come back to me. I will give you the best of the land in Egypt, and you will enjoy the fat of the land.' Tell them also: 'Take Egyptian wagons with you for your wives and little ones and bring their father with them. Give no thought to leaving your possessions behind; the best of all the land of Egypt will be yours.'" (vv. 16–20)

Pharaoh promises to take care of Jacob and his household. He dispatches carts to leave immediately to bring the family back to Egypt. And before they leave, Joseph gives all the brothers new clothing, "and to Benjamin he also gave three hundred pieces of silver and five sets of garments" (v. 22). His brothers had taken Joseph's robe, but he gives them new ones. And for his father, Jacob, he sent a variety of gifts and provisions for their journey. Joseph was a generous man, blessing others with the blessing that had been given to him.

"Then he sent his brothers off admonishing them, 'Don't quarrel along the way!'" (v. 24). Joseph had tasted first hand their tendency to quarrel and get angry. Having blessed Benjamin over the others, he was somewhat concerned that their jealousy might arise again on their way back home. Sounds like a real family, doesn't it?

Don't quarrel on the way! Perhaps Jesus said these words to his disciples as they walked the dusty trails together. Perhaps Jesus would say that to you today too. Are there any you have a quarrel with? Are there brothers or sisters you need to see differently, through the eyes of Jesus? We're to love one another, especially our family (Psalm 133:1).

LET'S PRAY

Father, I thank you for the people you have put in my life, my family, my friends, and even those who have once hurt me. I ask for grace today to be the most loving person in every room I walk into. Help me to speak words that give life and encourage others, always giving them grace and mercy when they might try to offend me. Thank you, God, for your grace on my life. Amen.

28

THE GOOD NEWS

[Joseph's brothers] left Egypt and went back home to their father
Jacob in Canaan. When they arrived, they ran to their father and
announced, "Joseph is still alive! Not only that, he is the ruler of all
Egypt!" The news so stunned Jacob that he nearly fainted. He could
not believe his ears! But when they told him all that Joseph had said
to them, and when he saw the wagons Joseph had sent to take him
to Egypt, he recovered from the shock. "My son Joseph is still alive!"
Israel said. "Now I'm convinced! I must go to see him before I die."
GENESIS 45:25–28

Imagine the scene as the eleven brothers arrive back home
to Jacob with their new clothes, new carts, donkeys, and all of
the other provisions. I can almost hear them exclaiming with a
loud voice, "Joseph is still alive!" Of course, Jacob was pleased
that Simeon was released and that Benjamin was with them, but

can you imagine what he must have felt when he heard the news about Joseph? He was stunned. The Hebrew text says, "His heart fainted!" In his mind and heart, he had buried Joseph years ago. Now he's told that his favorite son is alive and ruling over Egypt. What a gift! This was the best news of all. Joseph is alive! He would get to see him again.[10]

Have you wondered why Joseph didn't send for his father Jacob years earlier? Since Joseph was a ruler over Egypt, he could have sent chariots to Canaan before. And he could have shared his wealth and power long before then. Why then did he wait all that time until they showed up at his doorstep? Was it because he didn't care? No, Joseph cared deeply for his family...something else kept him back. Joseph was a man who chose to bear the pain of separation from his father rather than run ahead of God.

Joseph was an enthroned prince, yet he placed God's interests over his own. He knew that the plan of God must be fulfilled, not just the desires of Joseph. So he waited and waited again. Instead of initiating contact with his father and brothers, he stayed within the timing of the Lord. More than anything else, Joseph longed to see his father, but for nine years he did nothing. Even when the time came, he himself did not go; he waited until the others brought Jacob back. He was restricted to the will of God. This is why Joseph was a ruler and a prince. If you are unable to rule yourself, you will not be a good ruler over others.

Joseph was a man of God, a man who preferred to wait upon God, rather than initiate anything. Joseph was a man who denied his own emotions and flesh and chose to wait rather than to run ahead of God. At each step, he sought the Lord and found him. Instead of initiating contact with his dad, he stayed under the timing of the Lord. Even when it was in his power, Joseph waited nine years before God saw fit to remove his loneliness. The dreams of his youth included Jacob, his father, bowing before him also.

And Jacob's response shows a sign of true maturity in this aged patriarch, for there isn't a hint of blame when he heard the news of Joseph. His sons had lied to him, yet he didn't blame them.

JACOB LEAVES THE PROMISED LAND

"Israel packed up all he had and went to Beersheba where he offered sacrifices to the God of his father Isaac" (46:1). Jacob packed up and took everything, including every promise that God had ever given him, and he left for Egypt. Stopping in Beersheba was a significant stop for him. It was here that Abraham and Isaac had lived years before. And it was in Beersheba that Abraham planted the tamarisk tree and called upon the name of the Lord (21:33). So did Isaac (26:25). Jacob pauses here to offer sacrifices "to the God of his father Isaac." It was important for him to go to Beersheba to worship before he went on to Egypt.

Remembering the covenant of his fathers, Jacob worshiped the living God. He was leaving the land of promise. He was leaving it all behind and putting all that he had on the altar, so to speak. Every dream, every prophetic word, every hope of the promises being fulfilled, he left it all on the altar to be burned. The "Isaac" of his future destiny was left there.

There are times you, too, must leave everything behind to follow the plan of God. Even if it looks like your "destiny" will never be fulfilled. God knows what he is doing in your life, and he knows that separating your life for him alone is the only way for your dream to be fulfilled.

LET'S PRAY

Lord, I will leave behind whatever I must in order to follow you. Take my life, Lord, lead me. Your will is my pleasure. Your plan is my destiny. Teach me to love your ways as much as I love your presence. Amen.

29

To Egypt

God spoke to him in visions of the night, and called, "Jacob, Jacob!"
"Yes, I'm here," he answered. "I am God, the God of your father.
Do not be afraid to go to Egypt; for I will make your descendants
a great nation there. I will go with you to Egypt, and I will bring
your descendants back to this land. And the hand of Joseph will be
there to close your eyes when you die."[11] Then Jacob set out from
Beersheba. His sons put him, their little ones, and their wives in the
wagons that Pharaoh had sent.

GENESIS 46:2-5

Yahweh once again visits Jacob in the night and calls his name. Worship in total abandonment to God will lead to fresh revelation. "God...called, 'Jacob, Jacob!'" For the first time in twenty-two years the Lord appears to him and says, "I am God, the God of your father. Do not be afraid to go to Egypt." God reassured his servant that this journey to Egypt was the sovereign plan for his seed and his spiritual seed after him.

There is no mention of how long they would remain in Egypt or how large a nation they would become. All Jacob needed to know was that God was going with him. This is what comforts our hearts, knowing that our Lord is walking with us. That's all we need. We don't need all the answers, and we don't need to know all of our future ahead of time if we know that the Lord goes with us.

The Lord restores the communion that Jacob had once known. This divine encounter happened when Jacob was 130 years old (47:9). He was not afraid of a new challenge or new transition in his life. It was God's final promise to Jacob that they would return to the land of promise. God would someday bring all the Hebrews back into Canaan, and the bones of Jacob would come with them. And God promises Jacob that his beloved son, Joseph, would be there at his death.

Can you see a picture of old Jacob being carried into Egypt in a cart? Alongside of him are his eleven sons, their wives and children, their livestock and possessions. What a caravan! The whole number that went down to Egypt was sixty-six, to which you can add Joseph, his wife and two sons, for a total of seventy.[12] Can you imagine how the brothers felt as they made their journey to Egypt together? Joseph's dream was coming true.

JACOB'S REUNION WITH JOSEPH

Jacob sent Judah ahead to ask Joseph to lead them to Goshen. When they arrived, Joseph got in his chariot and rode to Goshen to meet his father, Israel. As soon as Joseph saw his father, he threw his arms around his father's neck and wept for a long time. Israel said to

Joseph, "I am ready to die, now that I have seen you and know that you are still alive." (46:28–30)

Jacob sends Judah to ask directions from Joseph. But Joseph didn't just give directions, he jumped in his chariot to go out and meet his father. Joseph had waited for this day for far too long. Then comes the incredible moment, a scene where words fail to fully describe the emotion involved, the moment when they embrace as father and son. Joseph "threw his arms around his father's neck and wept for a long time." This great Egyptian lord became a boy once more who needed the love of his father.

After two decades, Joseph finally gets to embrace the one man he had missed the most. The two men stood, staring into each other's eyes weeping. What a family reunion this was! However, it's nothing compared to the grand family reunion that we'll experience one day as we stand together before the One we love the most, Jesus.

We all need a father's love. I thank God that he has adopted us into his family. What joy and relief it is to know that he has accepted us into his family as his very own sons and daughters. Can you imagine what a wonderful family reunion awaits you in heaven? Those believing loved ones who have passed on are waiting for you to join them one day. It will be a reunion of joy, blessing, and bliss.

LET'S PRAY

Father, my heart aches at times to be with you and to see your Son face-to-face. And to be joined to those I love brings such warmth and comfort to my heart. Help me to live the remainder of my days in your paths of holiness and peace. I love you, Lord. Amen.

30

MEETING PHARAOH

Jacob gave Pharaoh a blessing.

GENESIS 47:7

Finally, the day came when Joseph introduced his brothers and father to Pharaoh. And although Pharaoh was the highest person on earth at that time, Pharaoh came under the blessing hand of Jacob. Jacob blessed Pharaoh, not vice versa. This refugee from Canaan became the "blesser" of this powerful world leader. And the fact that Jacob blessed Pharaoh proves that he was greater than Pharaoh (Hebrews 7:7). And Jacob moved in the authority of a prophet as he blessed him one more time as he was leaving.

In this chapter of Genesis, we see the abundance of God's provision for his people. Even in a time of a worldwide famine, Father God takes care of his people. The friends of God will be well provided for. And not only were Jacob and his sons provided for, but Joseph's brothers also received promotion and honor as they became the official herdsmen of Egypt.

The wealth of Egypt came streaming into Pharaoh's treasury through the wisdom and administration of Joseph. First their money, then their livestock, then their land until finally the Egyptians gave themselves to Pharaoh as servants. This was perhaps one of the greatest transferences of wealth in human history. This is important to note. For later on when God's people make their Exodus from Egypt, this is the wealth that they'll take with them. God used Joseph to make Egypt rich, and in time, Egypt would give it back to God's people. And with interest.

Joseph had a stellar reputation before Pharaoh. He never abused his authority. He could have hoarded up wealth for himself, but instead, he served Pharaoh faithfully. Even when the people came and begged him to "buy" them as slaves, he resisted the temptation to become opportunistic. He was a man of integrity and honor. He was great in the hour of temptation and great in the trials in Egypt. And he was greatest of all in his prosperity, after his dreams had come true. He was a man who could be trusted—totally trusted. He honored Potiphar and his wife. He honored Pharaoh. He honored his brothers who had betrayed him. In addition, he honored his father, even to his grave.

JOSEPH'S PROMISE TO JACOB

Israel and his descendants settled in Egypt in the land of Goshen. They had many children and multiplied, and they acquired property. Jacob lived in Egypt for seventeen years and lived a total of one hundred and forty-seven years. When the time of Israel's death was near, he summoned his beloved son Joseph and said to him, "Son, do me this favor before I die: Place your hand under my thigh as a pledge that you will show me kindness and loyal love. Do not bury me in Egypt, but when I go to rest with my fathers, I want you to carry me out of Egypt and bury me where they are buried. Swear that you will do this." So, Joseph took the oath and said, "I will do as you say." Then Israel worshiped and leaned on the top of his staff. (Genesis 47:27–31)

The entire time Egypt's wealth was being turned over to Pharaoh, Jacob lived in ease and comfort in Goshen. Even after the famine, Jacob lived for a total of seventeen years in Egypt with his family near him. And finally, the day came when the prince with God, Israel, was nearing death.

The one who prevailed over the angel had to submit to death just like all of us. He was 147 when he insisted that Joseph swear that his bones be carried out of Egypt and buried in the land of promise with his fathers. Why did all of this matter so much to Jacob? Abraham, Isaac, and Jacob were all buried near the ancient site of Jerusalem, where many centuries later Jesus would be crucified, buried, and raised from the dead. And Jacob was looking forward to the time of resurrection.

On the day Jesus was nailed to the cross, Scripture tells us, "Graves were opened. Then many of the holy ones who had died were brought back to life and came out of their graves. And after Jesus' resurrection, they were plainly seen by many people walking in Jerusalem" (Matthew 27:52–53).

Jacob was carrying the dreams of his father Abraham. He looked for a city whose maker and builder was God. In faith, he asked for a resting place near the spot where the Messiah would be crucified. And God honored that faith and raised many "holy people" to life in order to glimpse that city they had only dreamed of. And Jacob knew that the fulfillment of the promise would be in Canaan, not Egypt.

"So Joseph took the oath and said, 'I will do as you say.' Then Israel worshiped and leaned on the top of his staff." In worship and awe of the favor of Yahweh, Israel, limping Israel, leaned on the top of his staff. Perhaps Jacob remembered how good God had been to him. And he worshiped the Lord in his final days. Who knows what visions came to him during this anointed worship? Perhaps it was during this worship time that Jacob had an open vision of what would transpire in the lives of his sons and grandsons.

LET'S PRAY

Father, I want to worship you in every season of my life. In seasons of difficulty and in seasons of joy. Give me grace today, supernatural grace, to worship and praise you no matter what may come to distract me. I offer you my heart, my life, my all. Amen.

31

EPHRAIM AND MANASSEH

When Israel noticed Joseph's two sons, he said, "Who are these?"
"They are the sons that God has graciously given me here," Joseph
said to his father. "Please bring them closer," he said, "so that I may
bless them."

GENESIS 48:8–9

The bedridden Jacob knew that the end of his life was near. And when Joseph got word of it, he came with his two sons, Ephraim and Manasseh, to be with his father at his bedside. And as Joseph walked into the room, Jacob mustered enough strength to sit up on the side of his bed to talk with him. And like the dying man that he was, he began to share his heart with Joseph telling him all about a divine encounter he had in Bethel (Luz) and reminded him of the blessing El Shaddai, his God Almighty, had spoken over him. And he told him of the prophetic promises that the Father had revealed in that divine encounter. He knew that his time was about to end, and he needed to tell Joseph before it was too late. He wanted to transfer these prophetic promises on to Joseph, whom he had decided to deem as his firstborn. He knew that he needed to adopt Joseph's sons into the blessing of his inheritance as well. Israel wanted to transfer the blessing that unites generations to Joseph's sons.

And so Jacob spoke over Joseph that God would multiply his seed and that his sons would also have an inheritance in the land. For the Lord was adopting Joseph's sons as inheritors of the blessing. And just as Joseph replaced Reuben as the firstborn (Genesis 49:3–4; 1 Chronicles 5:2), Joseph's two sons would replace Jacob's second and third sons (Levi and Simeon).[13] And Joseph's two sons would enjoy equal status as Jacob's first two sons. Manasseh and Ephraim would never forget that moment.

"Now Israel could barely see, for his eyes were failing because of old age. So, Joseph brought his sons closer to him, and Joseph's father, their grandfather, hugged and kissed them" (Genesis 48:10). Jacob's blessing of the sons of Joseph is listed as his one supreme act of faith, for it demonstrated his unwavering confidence in the covenant promises of God. "Jacob worshiped in faith's reality at the end of his life, and leaning upon his staff he imparted a prophetic blessing upon each of Joseph's sons" (Hebrews 11:21).

This was one event Jacob never thought would happen. It followed his deepest grief and released his deepest joy. This was a demonstration that God can turn sorrow into joy. The Lord would be faithful to Joseph's sons, just as he was faithful to Joseph and just as he had been faithful to Jacob, Isaac, and Abraham.

These two sons were not infants, most likely they were teenagers. Joseph brought Ephraim and Manasseh to stand between

Jacob's knees, a ritual action declaring them his own issue. This "adoption" act touched Joseph so powerfully that he bowed his face to the ground before his father. And although Jacob was going blind, his spirit was clear. He had heard the prophetic stirring of God's Spirit within him. It was time to bless his grandchildren.

So as Joseph presented his sons to Jacob, he placed Manasseh, his firstborn, at Jacob's right hand. Joseph wanted to be sure his firstborn son received the blessing. And he was expecting for Ephraim to receive the blessing by Jacob's left hand. But, led by God, Jacob crossed his hands and placed his right hand of favor upon Ephraim's head and placed his left hand on Manasseh. And Joseph, not being pleased with this, tried to redirect Jacob's hands. But before Joseph could do anything Jacob begins to prophesy his blessing. And as the Spirit of prophecy fell upon Jacob, Joseph knew that it was God's will to bless and honor Ephraim above his brother Manasseh. The younger was set above the older and received a greater blessing and a greater work.

The Lord's blessing crossed over man's maneuvering. Blessing will always win out over maneuvering and posturing for favor. Maneuvering is our choosing, our selecting. Blessing is God's choice. It had taken Jacob a lifetime to learn this lesson: it is far better to wait until the blessing of God is seen and give up our maneuvering to have our own way.

Do you think Saul of Tarsus was thought of as the one God would bless? Nevertheless, as Saul was on his way to Damascus, the Lord guided his hand of blessing to fall upon this enemy of the church. I doubt that any of us would have picked Saul. But God did so that he might bless him. Even with our own children, we often do not know which one it is the Lord is about to bless. Perhaps even now, the hand of the Lord is crossing over to bless you.

And so Ephraim and Manasseh became strong leaders in Israel. Their descendants multiplied and grew mighty. Joshua was of the tribe of Ephraim, and so was Jeroboam. But the Jordan divided the tribe of Manasseh with one half on one side and the other half on the other side of the river, which made it less powerful. This is why Jacob crossed his hands. This blessing spoken by Jacob endured and still endures. When the Lord blesses, no one can turn it aside. Jacob's hands deceived and grasped what was not his, but now his hands were hands of blessing out of an overflow of life. The "heel-holder" has become the "blessing-giver." The day will come when this transformation will take place in you as well.

Let's Pray

> Lord, your ways are mysterious and beyond finding out. I love you. Thank you for choosing me to serve you and for the blessing of heaven that is on my life. Show me today how I can bless others as you have blessed me. Give me grace to sense your presence each moment as I walk with you today. Amen.

32

PROPHETIC BLESSING

Jacob called all his sons together and gathered them around his bedside. He said to them, "Let me prophesy to you about your future destinies."[14]

GENESIS 49:1

The aged Jacob gathers his strength, sits up in his bed, and speaks a prophetic blessing over his sons before he passes on. His sons born from four different mothers gather respectfully around his bed to hear his parting words. Previously, his words were deceitful, self-serving, and for self-gain. But now, the mature prophet speaks an enduring blessing over his boys. The struggle between flesh and spirit had been fierce and protracted in Jacob, but as the end draws near, he ministers from a deep well. The Spirit of prophecy falls upon him, and Jacob becomes a shaper of destiny for his children.

God revealed the future to his servant Jacob. Through prophetic revelation, Jacob could see the type of character each tribe would display. He spoke into their destiny and described God's plan for each one.

"Reuben, my firstborn, you are my strength and the firstfruits of my manhood. You are preeminent in pride and surpassing others in power" (vv. 3–4). As the firstborn, Reuben had the preeminence in dignity and honor. The natural blessings would be his, but he lost his supernatural birthright. He was gifted and favored but did not walk in integrity. Reuben was the might of his father, the firstfruits of Jacob's manhood.[15] As the first of many, he should have carried the mantle of favor but lost it because of defilement and corruption.

But Reuben's old sin finally catches up with him. "You are unstable—as turbulent as flood waters; you will no longer excel, for you have slept with my concubine and defiled yourself in your father's bed!" (v. 4). Reuben was unstable and "turbulent." His nature was not one of dignity and righteousness. He took what was not his and allowed lust to boil over. His ungoverned impulses and indulgences with his father's concubine, Bilhah, caused him to lose his birthright (Genesis 35:22; 1 Chronicles 5:1). Reuben had a destiny to be a prince but lost it by being promiscuous. It's possible to be one who excels in honor but be as uncontrolled as water. There must be an inner fortitude that withstands the tests of life. Natural abilities and a charming personality do not lead to bearing the fruit of the Spirit. Reuben may have been one who "surpassed others in power," but God's strength is made perfect in weakness.

There is no mention of a judge, prophet, or king ever listed from the tribe of Reuben. The armies of Reuben refused to heed the call of Deborah and Barak when they fought the Philistines.

The only notable ones in the whole tribe of Reuben were Dathan and Abiram, and their rebellion made then notable. They rebelled against Moses, causing the death of thousands. The tribe of Reuben settled on the wilderness side of Jordan (Numbers 32:1–5). And at no point did Reuben excel. His dignity and birthright were gone. He should have become a strong man with dignity and leadership authority; instead, he turned out to be a weak man who disgraced his family.

Don't ever think that immorality is a small matter with God. For we are made in God's image and made for purity, not lust. And fornication causes direct damage to our physical body, a vessel of honor made by God (1 Corinthians 6:8; 1 Thessalonians 4:4). As those who have been born again, we're now the holy temple of God's presence (1 Corinthians 6:19), purified and undefiled, and are to keep our vessel, our body, in an honorable way. Reuben lost the preeminence of his birthright because of this one sin he committed forty years earlier. Apostle Paul warns us that no fornicator, or immoral person, will have a birthright in the kingdom of God (1 Corinthians 6:9–10; Galatians 5:19–21; Ephesians 5:5).

Joseph received the birthright because he fled from the very defilement Reuben indulged in (Genesis 39:7–12). Joseph didn't lie down with Potiphar's wife, even when she begged him to. Joseph gained by purity what Reuben lost by defilement. This birthright was not only the double portion of land and possessions but also the privileges of headship and priesthood. Reuben lost it all, even though he likely repented and received a pardon. Sinful acts can disqualify us for spiritual privilege and leadership. You may be first in line for the blessing, but it's how you finish that counts.

Let's Pray

Father, I want to finish well. I want to be faithful and true to you as long as I live. Give me grace to finish my race. I want my life to be a message to others of your abundant grace and how you can restore my life and fill me with your fullness. Amen.

33

SIMEON AND LEVI

"Simeon and Levi, you are two of a kind and brothers in crime, for your swords have committed violent acts. O my soul, let me not join in their secret plans. O my heart, never let me be counted in their assembly, for they killed men in fits of rage, and for pleasure, they maimed an ox. Cursed be their anger, for it is fierce, and their wrath so relentless. I will divide your descendants throughout Jacob's territory and scatter them throughout Israel."

GENESIS 49:5-7

Simeon and Levi were next in age to Reuben but had brought grief and shame to their father Jacob. Neither Simeon nor Levi would be chosen to replace Reuben as the firstborn, for they were men of anarchy, not righteousness. Their angry disposition frightened Jacob.

Both Simeon and Levi had a disposition to kill others. Instead of using their swords for self-defense, they used their weapons to harm others. They had avenged the rape of their sister Dinah and also cruelly slaughtered and plundered the city of Shechem. Therefore, they received no blessing (34:25–30).

The Scripture teaches us to avoid foolish and violent men. And Proverbs warns us to "stay far away from them" (1:15). We walk under a curse when we walk in anger. Blowing your stack may seem human, but Scripture teaches, "Human anger is never a legitimate tool to promote God's righteous purpose" (James 1:20).

Simeon and Levi were not cursed, only their anger. For anger is the cause of many evils and will invite the judgment of God. "Don't let anger control you or be fuel for revenge, not for even a day" (Ephesians 4:26). Anger will keep you from the blessing of God. And part of the curse involves a scattering. Jacob knew that the two brothers could not dwell together. They weren't good for each other, so they were scattered. Anger scatters; humility unites.

Although Simeon and Levi were companions in violence, their descendants took different paths. Simeon continued to walk in unbridled passions. By all accounts, Simeon was the fiercest of the tribes of Israel.

The course of Simeon, like that of Reuben, was first downward and then upward. Ezekiel describes the final division of the land when there was finally a portion for Simeon. The tribe of Simeon is one of the sealed tribes mentioned in Revelation 7:7. And there is also a gate in the eternal city that has the name of Simeon inscribed upon it. God the Father is a redemptive God.

When Moses came down from the mountain with the two tablets of the law and found the people worshiping a golden calf, he said, "Whoever is for the Lord, come to me" (Exodus 32:26 NIV). Out of all the tribes, only one rallied to Moses, and that one tribe was the Levites. God used their killing disposition and had them strap a sword to their side to go among the camp and kill all who were worshiping the demonic idol.

The Levites killed three thousand of their own people. For this, the Lord set them apart as a people who would live wholly for the Lord. It seems the Levites' devotion to the Lord and willingness to lay aside the flesh reversed the curse that Jacob spoke over their anger. For each of the twelve tribes later had to set aside an allotment of cities for the Levites (Numbers 35:2–6). Altogether, the Levites were dispersed throughout the land in forty-eight cities, six of which were to be cities of refuge (Joshua 20:7–9). The Levites brought people to God and brought God to the people. And having Levites in your city was considered a blessing (Judges 17:7–13).

God's grace always triumphs over darkness. Maybe you think that God can't use your natural disposition. But that's far from the truth. It can be used by him to go against your own natural desires in a sanctified and transformed way. You might be very strong-willed. God still uses those who are strong-willed after they have been broken and crucified with Christ. We must be set apart from our natural tendencies and broken by the dealings of God. Then once we have been redeemed by the blood, our hearts are transformed. Then God the Father can and will use us and our natural tendencies the way they were meant to be used as we continue to yield to him. He is a redeeming God.

Because Levi's natural ways underwent a transformation, he carried God's Urim and Thummim as a priest. Levites had the wonderful privilege of serving God in his presence. Their inheritance was not a piece of land but the privileges of intimate worship of Yahweh. We learn much from the story of the Levites. God can redeem and transform us, even after we've lost the blessing by our past failures.

Moses, the author of Genesis, was from the tribe of Levi. Do not even think of your past as it relates to God, for your past ended two thousand years ago with three nails. Now, you have only a destiny.

LET'S PRAY

Father, I thank you for washing my soul clean in the blood of Jesus. I thank you that anger will not hide in my soul any longer. I want to be a pure and holy priest in your presence. Set me apart today for your glory. Amen.

34

JUDAH

*"O Judah, your brothers will praise you. You will conquer your foes
in battle, and your father's sons will bow down before you."*

GENESIS 49:8

What glorious things Jacob speaks of Judah! Blessings would
overflow to this one whose name means "he will be praised." Even
his siblings would praise him. You know it's God's favor when your
brothers bless and honor you. It was the birth of Judah that caused
Leah to say, "This time I will praise the Lord." The child that
brought praises to God will receive his brothers' praises one day.

It is also prophesied that Judah would be victorious and conquer his enemies, achieving great triumph. His "father's sons will
bow down" to him because of his great victory. Jacob saw in the
Spirit, blessing honor and power descending upon his son, Judah.

He would be a strong and courageous leader with others showing him great respect.

Judah was the founder of the royal tribe that would one day bring forth the Lion of Judah, Christ Jesus, the Messiah. And the tribe of Judah produced many kings; some were quite notable in their exploits for God and were a conquering and ruling tribe.

Judah was to have the leadership among his brothers. Jesus Christ, from the tribe of Judah, would one day receive all the praises of his brothers in Israel. Judah is a wonderful picture of this One who we see as the mighty Lion of Judah. And true to the prophetic word of Jacob, Jesus Christ is the one who has conquered every foe in battle.

"Judah, my son, you are like a young lion, who has devoured its prey and departed. Like a lion, he crouches and lies down, and like a lioness—who dares to awaken him?" (Genesis 49:9). What a wonderful picture this is of our Lord Jesus Christ, the Lion of the tribe of Judah (Revelation 5:5). This is more than a prophecy of the tribe of Judah becoming strong and mighty; it's a prophecy of the One who will come from Judah to devour his prey. Jesus is not a raging Lion; he's a resting Lion who has conquered every foe. He has crouched, but now he lies down in perfect peace. His victory is total and secure. Who would dare rouse a lion when he is lying down after his kill? And who would rouse a lioness while she is guarding her cubs?

Jesus came as our Savior ("a young lion"). He went to the cross and destroyed the one who held us in fear of death and rose again to take a seat at God's right hand ("Like a lion he crouches and lies down"). Today, he is guarding us with tender love and compassion ("like a lioness"). Christ was the young lion crouching as he waited for his prey. After seizing his prey, Jesus Christ brought captivity captive and took us all with him on high where we've been seated together in him. He has conquered the devil and has conquered us. It's time to experience him as the resting Lion, victorious and satisfied. When we do, we'll become like a lioness and give birth to many cubs. The church is lion country—and everyone born of him is a lion cub. Toward men we are lambs following the Lamb, but toward Satan we are lion cubs following *the* Lion.

"The scepter of rulership will not be taken from Judah, nor the ruler's staff from his descendants, until the Shiloh comes and takes what is due him, for the obedience of nations belongs to him" (Genesis 49:10). Jacob foresees the coming of Shiloh. The phrase "until the Shiloh comes" can also be translated "to whom it belongs comes." Jesus is the One to whom everything rightfully belongs (Ezekiel 21:27). Shiloh becomes a symbolic name for the coming Messiah.

This is a clear prophecy that Messiah would be from the tribe of Judah. The scepter he holds is the rod of authority to rule over nations. The King of our hearts has all authority to govern our souls and lead our lives into his perfect plan. Can you see Jesus as your King today holding the "scepter of rulership" over your life? As one who has been born from above, you are his true descendant. His ruler's staff is now in your hands. God has sent you into the world as a prince or princess to extend his kingdom and reveal his glory. Your life will be a witness for the King.

LET'S PRAY

Almighty God, you have anointed your Son, Jesus Christ, to rule over all things. I ask that your kingdom come into my life and my family. May your Spirit guide my steps today in your righteous paths. Help me to see your grace and power conquer every foe that stands before me. I take your hand, my King and my God. Amen.

35

ZEBULUN, ISSACHAR, AND DAN

*"Zebulun will settle along the seashore
and become a safe harbor for ships."*

GENESIS 49:13

The twelve tribes of Israel came from the twelve sons of Jacob. Each received a prophetic word of destiny before their father died. Having spoken of the tribe from which Jesus was born (Judah), Jacob now continues to prophesy of the tribe in whose territory Christ lived. It was there that Christ began his ministry, the area settled by Zebulun. The people of Zebulun were the first to see this great light dawning. And the disciples of Galilee carried the light of the gospel to the peoples. They would take the gospel out and rejoice greatly as they reached people with the message of eternal life. It was from a mountain top in Galilee that Jesus sent out his disciples to the nations. As the Galileans went out with the good news of the gospel tidings, they became havens of refuge to many.

ISSACHAR

The smallest, least mentioned tribe in the Bible is Issachar. They were not dominant or prestigious like Judah, from which King David and our Lord Jesus Christ came. They were not prosperous like Ephraim, which boasted leaders like Joshua and Samuel. They were not the strong tribe like Dan that produced a Samson. And they were not a special tribe like Levi, the priestly one. They had no great history. They were nobodies.

"Issachar is a strong donkey lying down between its saddle-bags" (v. 14). How would you like to receive a prophetic word like that? The sons of Issachar are donkeys. They are burden bearers. A horse loves speed, but a donkey is made for carrying burdens. A donkey is focused and sure-footed when it walks on mountain heights. A horse needs blinders, or it can become easily distracted. But a donkey keeps its attention on the trail ahead. A donkey can endure weeks of hard conditions with little rest. Sounds like an intercessor. The men of Issachar are noted in Scripture as those "who understood the times and knew what Israel should do" (1 Chronicles 12:32 NIV). They become the counterpart to the end time intercessor of today.

Issachar is truly a picture of a true intercessor. Like the donkey that carried Jesus into Jerusalem, they are not only willing but also able to carry burdens because their prayer-partner is Christ. Could it be that intercessors are those whom God has chosen to "carry" his presence into the nations? We are to loose them, for the Master has need of them.

Dan

"Dan will provide justice for his people, as one of the tribes of Israel" (Genesis 49:16). The name Dan means "judge" or "he who provides justice." The tribe of Dan was to have a destiny of providing justice, to become like the conscience of the nation. Although smaller than the other tribes, they were to excel in helping against the suppression of an enemy.

What potential we each have to bless or hinder God's people! Each prophecy Jacob spoke released authority. The Hebrew word for "tribe" is literally *scepter*, which is a symbol of authority. And they must always be used for blessing not cursing.

During this prophecy over his sons, Jacob exclaims, "I wait in hope for your salvation, O Yahweh!" (v. 18) Why would he say this? Was he just asking for strength to finish his prophetic utterances? The Hebrew word for "salvation" is *Yeshua*; the Greek form is *Jesus*. Jacob was looking to the end of the ages and saw the coming of Jesus. The true judge of all the earth, who alone will provide justice for his people, is the Lord Jesus Christ. The salvation or deliverance Jacob waited for was Christ, the promised seed. Dan may fail, but Jesus will succeed in leading us into the salvation, the deliverance of the Lord.

In 1 Chronicles 2–9 we find that the tribe of Dan is omitted in the record of God's holy people. Neither is he mentioned in the record of Revelation 7. The sin of idolatry caused his name to be blotted out. Nevertheless, the "deliverance" of the Lord steps in. The prophet Ezekiel does list Dan's tribe as one of the glorious inheritors of God's promises (Ezekiel 48:1). Mercy triumphs over judgment.

Let's Pray

God, I love to call you Father! You have made me your child. I am yours today and every day. Give me a prayer today that I can bring before you and bless someone else. Help me to go and do today what you would want me to do. And help me to stand for justice and truth. With your grace, I can do all things. Amen.

36

GAD, ASHER, AND NAPHTALI

*"Gad will be raided by raiders, but he will raid at their heels
and overcome them at last."*

GENESIS 49:19

This is a word play on the name *Gad* using variations in the Hebrew. The words *raid* and *raiders* are both amazingly similar to the name Gad. Scholars tell us that his name can mean either "good fortune" or "band of raiders." Although raiders will attack Gad, Gad will fight valiantly. He will chase them away, attacking them as they flee ("at their heels").

Some facts about the tribe of Gad:

- Moses, the law-giver, was buried in the land of Gad.

- Gad was the sixth stone on the breastplate, a diamond.

- Historically, Gad's blessing was that he would be enlarged, choosing the best portion, and would obtain victory over his enemies.

- Although the tribe of Gad received land on the fertile plain of the Jordan, they went on into the land and fought alongside their brothers to help them conquer their portion.

Asher

"Asher's food will be rich, and he will provide delicacies fit for a king" (v. 20). How would you like a prophetic word like this spoken over you? Asher's portion would be blessed with royal dainties. Out of the victory of Christ, Asher's portion is yours. In Christ, we feast on food fit for kings, for we belong to his royal family. Truly, grace has blessed us. In Christ, a kingly family has adopted us, and we have royal dining privileges.

Moses' prophecy about Asher is incredible: "Most blessed of sons is Asher; let him be favored by his brothers, and let him bathe his feet in oil" (Deuteronomy 33:24 NIV). Asher would receive great favor from his brothers. The Lord is the One who exalts and lifts up. Who could not honor those whom the Lord blesses?

Oil soaked feet speaks of walking in the anointing and richness of the Holy Spirit. He and his footprints would be in oil, releasing the oil of gladness. Everywhere he walked he would receive the blessing of the Holy Spirit. Does that describe you? It's time to have your feet soaked in oil, the precious oil of Holy Spirit (Psalm 133).

And the name *Asher* means "blessed" or "happy." Hasn't the Lord blessed you and made you happy? In Christ we have limitless blessings (Ephesians 1:3) and joy overflowing in the Holy Spirit. The tribe of Asher settled in one of the most fertile places in the land and became exporters of oil and crops. Blessings abounded to them, and blessings abound to us.

NAPHTALI

"Naphtali is a doe set free, who bestows beauty on his off-spring" (Genesis 49:21). A doe set free is such a beautiful word picture. Psalm 22 has as its inscription, "The doe of the morning." And in the Passion Translation, "The deer at the dawning of the day." We know this Psalm to be about our Lord Jesus in his death and resurrection. Jesus is the deer at the dawning of the day, the doe set free. His resurrection released him (and us) from the power of death. In Naphtali, we see Christ as the resurrected doe skipping on the mountaintops in freedom. Nothing will frustrate him, and no one needs to help him. He is the resurrected doe of the morning glory.

The resurrection of Christ has let loose God's people. The name *Naphtali* means "wrestling." Yet what freedom we experience when he pins us to the mat, and we get up a changed person. We may run to the mountains with him in victory, for he has paid the price for our freedom.

The phrase "who bestows beauty on his offspring" can also mean "that utters beautiful words." How lovely and powerful are the words of our resurrected doe. This could refer to the Great Commission of Matthew 28. When Jesus gathered his disciples together on a mountaintop, he sent them out with beautiful words, the good news to preach to all peoples. When we have tasted the resurrection, we have beautiful words to give others. We become his beautiful fawns. The doe set free. Have you been set free? Do you speak beautiful words over others?

LET'S PRAY

> Father, I am yours, and you are mine. Today, I set my life before you and ask that you make me a blessing to others. Open my eyes to see opportunities to encourage and help someone else. And give me grace to set others free from their pain and sorrow. In Jesus' name. Amen.

37

Joseph, a Fruitful Vine

"Joseph is a fruitful vine, a fruitful vine growing by a spring, whose branches run over a wall."

Genesis 49:22

The beloved Joseph, deliverer of his people, received a lengthy and powerful prophetic blessing from his father. He was called a "fruitful vine growing by a spring," or "by a fountain." The prophecies of Jacob's sons show the maturing of sonship. Joseph, the clearest type of Christ in the Old Testament, is seen as a fruitful vine. The Lord Jesus called himself the fruitful Vine and us his branches (John 15). When the fruitful Vine lives through us, our personality begins to show the fruit of the Spirit (Galatians 5:22–23). Jesus branches out through us, just as he branches out from the Father. Joseph was too busy being fruitful to be negative.

The "spring" or fountain is the life coming from Yeshua. This was Joseph's dwelling place and source of fruitfulness. He was planted by the spring of eternal life (Psalm 1:3). And this fruitful vine's branches ran over the wall. And today, Christ branches out through us as well, without restriction. Nothing will limit the branching forth of Christ in us when we walk in the Joseph anointing.

Even if you're taken into captivity to Egypt's dungeon, the springing well within you will cause your branches to climb over every barrier, and nothing will hem you in. The enemy will always try to restrict your fruitfulness, but Christ's life in you will overcome every obstacle.

> "Persecutors fiercely attacked; they pursued him with their bows and arrows. But Joseph's bow remained steady, because the power of the Mighty One of Jacob strengthened him, by the name of the loving Shepherd, the Rock of Israel." (Genesis 49:23–25)

Joseph was a man who suffered at the hands of his brothers. Like bitter archers, they attacked him and shot him with their arrows of jealousy and accusation. It seems the more fruitful and anointed we become, the more jealous opposition arises from among our brothers.

From the days of Cain and Abel until now, the heart of man cannot stand it when God favors another one above us. For everyone wants to be king, the one and only—God's chosen. And only to make matters worse, we discover that our very pride disqualifies us, and we begin to turn on those who have found their place of favor with the Father. This religious cycle of brother persecuting brother has to cease. For our loving Shepherd and Rock has a beautiful destiny waiting for each and every one of us. Then we can joyfully defer to God's wisdom and rejoice with those who rejoice. May we lay aside our arrows and honor our loving Shepherd and our Rock by honoring others.

Notice the beautiful way that God gives his strength to Joseph. The Hebrew is literally, "The arms of his hands were made strong by the hands of the mighty God of Jacob." God is pictured as putting his mighty hands on Joseph's hands, placing his arms on Joseph's arms. Like a father teaches his children, so the Lord teaches those who fear him. He puts his arms upon you so that you would be strengthened just like he did with Joseph.

And the sting of their bitterness did not defeat Joseph. Even while his brother shot at him with hostility, "Joseph's bow remained steady." He was able to overcome the hostility of angry brothers by holding onto the Lord in faith, which made his arms strong and steady. A holy confidence that God was enough for him kept Joseph pure. If the Lord is your Mighty One, you can leave vindication in his hands. But if your trust is in the flesh, then you'll constantly be trying to defend and protect your dignity. May the Mighty One be greater than your reputation. If he is your Shepherd, then you lie down and rest where the Lord has put you.

Let the Lord be your Shepherd, and you won't want anything else. Even in a prison cell, there's a joy that comes when he's your Shepherd and Rock. Hell may shoot its arrows at your soul, but heaven will shield you in grace. Throughout these continual attacks, you will only become stronger.

There are few things more difficult to endure than misunderstanding and persecution from our brothers and sisters in Christ. It's so much easier to understand opposition from the unbelievers, but when it comes from the household of faith, it tastes so bitter. They mocked Joseph, stripped him of his robe of favor, threw him in a pit, and betrayed him by selling him into slavery. God had to be his Shepherd and his Rock. And like Joseph, we, too, need our Shepherd to care for us and a Rock for us to stand on—God is always there for us. This Mighty One made Joseph strong. In times of persecution and hostility, we must find our strength in him and stand on him as our Rock.

Potiphar's house proved to be a repeat of all that he had already experienced. Potiphar's seductive wife was like a bitter archer shooting the poisonous arrows of false accusation at Joseph. In Scripture, the picture of shooting arrows is compared to bitter words lodging in our hearts (Psalm 57:4; 64:3–4; Proverbs 25:18). Joseph's brothers lied about him; Potiphar's wife lied about him; the archers shot mercilessly at Joseph. Yet God was the secret of his strength. Joseph did not shoot back. His bow of faith did not fail. Every servant of the Lord must walk in this Joseph anointing, becoming a picture of Jesus to others.

Have others ever told lies about you? It is a painful test, but with God's grace, you will pass that test and experience the same favor that was on Joseph's life.

LET'S PRAY

Father, I want to have a life that bears fruit and that excels in every way. Teach me your ways. Show me the path that leads to your pleasure. I want to advance in my relationship with you. Help me today to remove everything that might stand between us. I have no other God but you. I love you, Father. Amen.

38

A BLESSED LIFE

"The God of your Father will help and protect you; the God who
is more than enough will bless you. He will bless you with the
blessings of heaven, blessings of the deep that lie beneath, and
blessings of the breast and womb."

GENESIS 49:25

Jacob declares that God will pass the blessing that he has on his life upon Joseph's. Once again, we see the blessing uniting generations. The Lord is with Joseph, and the Lord is also with you. Our hope for the future is blessing, not calamity. God will be faithful to help you and bless you, just as he did with Joseph. The Almighty is the One who loves us and blesses us with heaven's favor. Heaven smiles upon you when you set the Lord before your heart. Every blessing in the heavenly places is yours to keep, young Joseph. In difficulties and dangers, the Lord will be there for you.

Subterranean springs will open up before you with "blessings of the deep that lie beneath." Blessings overflowing will be heaped upon Joseph and his descendants. His children will be born in safety and comfortably nursed.

> "The blessings of your father will be greater than the
> blessings of the eternal mountains, surpassing the
> blessings of my ancestors! May Joseph's blessings crown
> his head and rest on the brow of the one set apart, prince
> among his brothers." (v. 26)

What statements of blessing Jacob speaks over this faithful son! Jacob is leaving a spiritual mantle and legacy of favor to this tested one. Blessings older than the hills and as stable as the eternal mountains. The earth would bring its bounty to Joseph, "the best gifts of the earth and its fullness and the favor of him who dwelt in the burning bush" (Deuteronomy 33:16 NIV). All of these blessings would be like a crown on the head of a prince. The heart of Joseph was princely and noble. It was so fitting for Jacob to speak these blessings over Joseph. God had tested him, and he came through like gold refined in the fire.

Here is a catalog of blessings given to Joseph:

- Blessed with the blessings of heaven (peace, life, unity—Deuteronomy 33:14)

- Blessed with the blessings of the deep that lie beneath (anointings and promises of life and power—v. 16)

- Blessed with the blessings of the breast (sustaining grace in trials, revelation knowledge—v. 15)

- Blessed with the blessings of the womb (multiplying of life, fruitfulness, and abundance—v. 15)

- Blessed with the blessings of his father that will be greater than the blessings of the eternal mountains (authority, strength, and wealth—v. 15)

- Blessed with blessings surpassing the blessings of Jacob's ancestors (increased favor—v. 16)

- Blessed with blessings crowning his head and resting on his brow (wisdom—v. 16)

These are the very blessings that we, too, have been blessed with in the heavenly places in Christ Jesus (Ephesians 1:3). They are God's blessings to Christ and Christ's blessings to you. He's the same one who dwelt in the tabernacle in the wilderness, then in the temple of Solomon, and now he's dwelling in his church. But there's a day coming when he will dwell in us as a people called the Bridal City, his New Jerusalem.

BENJAMIN

"Benjamin is a ferocious wolf. He devours his prey; in the evening, he divides the spoil" (Genesis 49:27). Judah was a lion, Naphtali a doe, and now we have Benjamin the wolf. As a hungry wolf that can kill more than he can eat, Benjamin would devour the prey and have plenty left over for others. Its fierceness and ferocity define a wolf. Benjamin was the fiercest and most war-like of all the tribes. If ever there was a battle, Benjamin would be there (Judges 19:16; 2 Samuel 2:15–16; 1 Chronicles 8:40; 12:2). Ehud, the assassin, was of this tribe (Judges 3:15–22). Saul of Tarsus, who persecuted the church like a ravenous wolf, was also from the tribe of Benjamin.

Moses prophesied over the tribe of Benjamin: "Let the beloved of the Lord rest secure in him, for he shields him all day long, and the one the Lord loves rests between his shoulders" (Deuteronomy 33:12 NIV). Benjamin would be the beloved of the Lord. As a "son of my right hand"—you will also rest between his shoulders. So comfort your heart in this promise. To the enemy, Benjamin is a ravenous wolf, but to the Lord, he is the beloved one.

Benjamin dwelt between the two shoulders or two hills. And on one of the hills was Jerusalem, where the temple was located. The Lord's dwelling was a covering of love over Benjamin all the days of his life and all the days of your life too. And Jesus Christ is the true beloved One who rests between the shoulders of the Father. You, too, have a resting place between the shoulders of Jesus, over his heart. You can lean upon him no matter what you're going through. He calls you his beloved.[16]

LET'S PRAY

I love you, Lord! You have made me who I am. You have guarded and guided my life from the day I was born. You have never made a mistake with me. I rest between your shoulders, upon your heart. Let me feel your presence with me every moment of this day. Amen.

39

JACOB'S LAST WORDS

Afterward, Jacob sat on the side of his bed and instructed his sons with these words: "I am about to join my people in death. Bury me with my ancestors in the cave of the field of Ephron the Hittite—the cave in the field of Machpelah, near Mamre, in the land of Canaan. My grandfather Abraham purchased that field as a burial site from Ephron the Hittite. My grandfather Abraham and my grandmother Sarah are buried there. My father Isaac and my mother Rebekah were buried there also. And it is the place I buried my wife Leah. So, bury me there, in that cave, in the field that was purchased from the Hittites." When Jacob finished his final words of instruction to his sons, he lifted his feet onto the bed, breathed his last, and was gathered to his people.

GENESIS 49:29–33

Jacob now gives his sons a solemn charge concerning his burial. He asks them to take his body from Egypt to Canaan so that he could rest with his fathers in the cave in Canaan. This was not a sentimental request as much as an act of faith. Jacob knew that Canaan was the land of promise, the inheritance given to him from God. And so like Jacob, it's always good for us to keep in our minds and our hearts that our inheritance is not of this world, but we have a heavenly promised land, and we don't have to wait till we die to experience it. We have been given all in Christ, who is our spiritual inheritance, our promised land.

When he had finished speaking, Jacob was ready to leave this world for his heavenly Bethel where he would finally see the God of Bethel face-to-face in all his glory. Jacob lived to be 147 years old, but now he lives in eternal light with the Dayspring on high.

"Joseph flung himself over Jacob, kissing him and weeping. And his tears fell on his father's face" (50:1). A tender moment takes place as Joseph kisses his departed father with tears. Then he orders the Egyptian embalmers to prepare Jacob's body for burial and a forty-day grieving process. Even the Egyptians mourned for Jacob. The mourning period for a pharaoh was seventy-two days, and for Jacob, it was seventy days. Truly, they honored the aged patriarch, the father of their deliverer, Joseph.

Having obtained permission from Pharaoh to bury his father in Canaan land, Joseph sets out with the all the dignitaries of Egypt. Many chariots and horsemen—a huge entourage—accompanied Joseph to Canaan in a stately funeral procession.

This was Joseph's first trip back to his native land in thirty-nine years. Sadly, it was for his father's funeral. We can see the tender heart of Joseph weeping over his father again. They laid

Jacob to rest in the cave of Machpelah, and Joseph returns to his post in Egypt.

BURYING THE PAST

Jacob was gone. Only the children remained. How would Joseph now look at his brothers? This would be his chance to vent—to seek revenge for the miserable situations they had put him through. Joseph was in the royal court of Egypt, and so he could do as he wished. No one would stop him if he chose to eliminate these offending brothers. So Joseph's brethren humbly made their way to court his favor.

Again we see the character of this man Joseph. Gentle, tender, and forgiving. He'd suffered much and endured the pain of rejection from his own brothers. Yet we see him weeping repeatedly over the grief and shame of his brothers regarding what they had done to him. They had come to him with a manufactured message from Jacob. Their shame brought him to tears. Without hesitation, he offered them reassurance and forgiveness.

We see Joseph speaking kindly to those who hurt him and comforting their hearts. He refused to harbor a grudge or treat them even slightly differently because of what they had done. God dealt with the envy among brothers by turning the chosen brother into a spiritual father. When Joseph became like a father to his brothers, the envy issue was silenced, and they were free to relate to Joseph with honor.

"How could I ever take the place of God?" (50:19). Every time you are tempted to hold unforgiveness in your heart, you should ask this question. Only God can judge, for he has perfect love and knows all things. Since we are not in his place, we only have the right to forgive. Had Joseph been a lesser man, he would have filled the role of God. For many play the carnal game of "king of the mountain" when they have someone cornered and vulnerable. But Joseph refused to do that. He understood that God could turn the evil intentions of others into something good. God has power to transform pain into blessing when we love him through it all (Romans 8:28). A sovereign King will work through the pain to bring us into great blessing.

Waiting is the difficulty. In the hour of testing, we often forget the future good that will come as we remain faithful. God will work his glory through our life. Glory to Jesus and good for us will result as we love our way through life. None of life is a mistake or wasted when we have our eyes on the One who guides us. The cross was the greatest evil ever done to another. Yet from this horrible travesty came the most glorious salvation. God turned the evil deeds of men into a fountain of saving grace.

LET'S PRAY

Father, you work everything together for my good. My life is a testimony of your faithfulness. You have chosen me for greatness and set me apart to be your devoted follower. I love how you love me and empower me to walk with you. Set my heart on fire today so that I will never give up. Amen.

40

JOSEPH'S DEATH

"I will die one day, but God will certainly come to you and fulfill his promises to bring you and your descendants from this land and lead you to the land he promised to Abraham, Isaac, and Jacob."

GENESIS 50:24

Do you know why God exalted Joseph to greatness? It was because he had learned to love. None of us love naturally; we need divine empowerment. One way love manifests is through forgiving those who wound us. To love another is to totally forgive them. Do you love your enemies? We have so much to learn. Life is designed to teach us to love every time we're disappointed with someone else. God did not exalt Joseph until he had totally forgiven his brothers. And God will not exalt you until you do the same. What does true forgiveness look like?

When you have truly forgiven, you don't want the person to

be afraid of you. Joseph was moved by their fear and told them, "Don't be afraid" (v. 19). When you refuse to be friendly or want to capitalize on their offense in your relationship, you're showing a lack of love. That's not the way of the Father. God never gives you the cold shoulder when you come before his throne.

When you have truly forgiven, you see others as God's agents to teach you more of him. Joseph calmed their fears by these forgiving words: "Even though you intended to hurt me, God intended it for good" (v. 20). If you can see God at work, you'll not stumble over the misdeeds of others. Forgiveness will point your offenders to God's purpose, not merely what they've done against you. Vengeance cannot lodge in your heart if you have your eyes on God and eternity.

When you have truly forgiven, you keep on forgiving. To do it once is good, but you're not finished yet. You must keep your heart in a posture of continual forgiveness, seventy times seven. Joseph speaks incredible words over his brothers: "I myself will provide for you all that you need, both for you and your little ones" (v. 20). His forgiveness was going to last. Love would cover and protect them and their children. More than a burst of emotions, true forgiveness is an attitude that you will prove over time.

THE WAY TO LIVE, THE WAY TO DIE

To the very end of his life, Joseph was a joy to be around. He was forgiving, gracious, and kind. He was never complaining; he held no regrets and no bitterness. This is the way to live, and this is the way to die. Rather than pointing his family to what he had achieved, he pointed them to the enduring promises of God. At the rich old age of one hundred and ten, Joseph passed on to his reward and inheritance, leaving precious memories for all his loved ones. Truly, he was a man of integrity and grace. Before Joseph passed on, he instructed his family to carry his bones out of Egypt on their day of deliverance. Even in death, Joseph had his eyes fixed on eternity. Joseph was thinking of life beyond the grave. "Faith inspired Joseph and opened his eyes to see into the future, for as he was dying he prophesied about the exodus of Israel out of Egypt, and gave instructions that his bones were to be taken from Egypt with them" (Hebrews 11:22).

By his astonishing declaration about his bones, Joseph proclaimed he lived for the promises of God rather than temporal concerns; he refused to be identified with his successes, accomplishments, or the blessings on his life but only with the promises. He proclaimed that Egypt was not his home but that the promised land of Canaan was; he and they were but strangers and sojourners in the land of Egypt. His bones would become a "monument of temporality" to his descendants, reminding them that this life was to be but a warm-up for the life to come, and their promised inheritance was in the other life. Joseph had been a dreamer, and now he was a prophet when he said, "God will certainly come to you" (Genesis 50:24). He knew that the exodus was coming, and he didn't want to be left behind.

Genesis begins with God's command for light to illuminate the earth as it thrusts its way through the universe and ends with a coffin in Egypt. And so even though Genesis ends with this sad note, Joseph's promise leaves them with hope. But not only does Joseph impart hope to his brothers but to us also. Joseph was not only prophesying to his brothers but also to the seed that was yet to be born—you and me. Joseph was prophesying to all who are in Christ today. Genesis is but the beginning of the story of God's spiritual seed and firstfruits of the promise of a glorious destiny for you.

Let's Pray

Father God, you are the One who makes my dreams come true. You amaze me, my God. The way you have led my life is perfect, and I cannot complain. Everything you have done is right and true. Thank you for giving me your Son, your Spirit, and your life. I delight in following you. Help me for the rest of my life to trust in your grace and goodness. Amen.

THE TWELVE SONS OF JACOB

Before we leave this section of Scripture and the remarkable prophecy of Jacob it contains, we must see it as a picture of the Lord Jesus Christ and of our progression toward fullness in him. Each of these sons gives us a different aspect of Christ's life, and they each become a gateway for us in becoming the New Jerusalem (Revelation 21).

These twelve sons are the gateways to glory of the New Jerusalem (Psalm 24:7–9). Each gate was a stone, a jewel with the name of a son engraved upon it. What symbolism we can find in these twelve gateway-sons.

Among the twelve sons of Jacob, the first, Reuben, was a sinner, and the last, Benjamin, became the dwelling place of God. We are all headed toward a Benjamin experience of becoming a people of the Lord's right hand. We will pass through each of the meanings of the sons of Jacob, from Reuben to Benjamin, in our journey into the New Jerusalem reality. The twelve gates of the city carry the secrets of our journey into Christ. It maps out the process God takes us through in making us a dispenser of his life. "And those who possess his perfect righteousness he co-glorified with his Son!" (Romans 8:30).

If you put together the record of these twelve sons in Genesis 49, it reveals both the Christ and the church, his dwelling place. What a rich portion of God's Word!

1. **Reuben** means "Behold, a son!" The prophecy over Reuben points to the firstborn of all creation, our Lord Jesus Christ, whom we must receive as Savior. Our heavenly "Reuben" is excellent and worthy of our fervent gaze for endless days. As we study the meanings of the names of the twelve tribes in succession, from birth to full stature (Reuben–Benjamin), we begin to see a picture of what God is doing in us. Reuben speaks of the new birth, an impartation of the divine nature in seed form. To walk through the "Reuben Gate" is the beginning of our becoming the New Jerusalem. It is the experience of receiving Christ our Savior, of freedom from all our sins. The Reuben revelation is only the beginning of our new life in Christ. However, if all you know of him is the new birth, you'll remain unstable as water (Genesis 49:4). To be an overcomer, you must advance and pass through the other eleven gates (experiences) as well.

2. **Simeon** means "a hearing ear" or "the one who hears." Jesus Christ was the One who always heard his Father's voice and responded to him. In Christ, we receive a

hearing and a listening heart. As we are empowered (baptized) by the Holy Spirit, he opens our ears to hear the voice of God (Isaiah 50:4). We will hear the voice of the Lord in many ways and at different times. But simply hearing his voice doesn't make us like Christ; we must obey. Keep going on. Baptism in the Spirit is not enough. There are ten more gates waiting for you. If you stop there, you will only damage others by wrongly using your gift of hearing to divide and disperse. When we pass through the "Simeon Gate," we enter into the fullness (baptism) of the Spirit that releases grace to hear from God.

3. **Levi** means "to join, unite, attach." This clearly speaks of flowing together in ministry with God and man. Our hearts are joined in intimacy first, then in ministry. Because of Levi's zeal for the Lord when he refused to worship the golden calf after Israel's deliverance from Egypt, God rewarded the tribe of Levi by calling them to be his priests so that they would be "joined" to God and find God alone as their inheritance. Today there are those who realize they are the bride of Christ and are determined to live in union with him, joined to his heart. To be joined to the Lord is what qualifies us as his priests. To pass through the "Levi Gate" means that we intercede, we pray, we passionately join our hearts to Jesus Christ to serve his purposes. How God is waiting for you to pass through this gateway! We cannot become his eternal city until we are joined to him in Levitical

worship, worshiping in the holy place. And not only do we unite our hearts with the heart of Jesus, but we also must unite our hearts to others in the faith. We become like the winged cherubim in Ezekiel's vision that join their wings to each other. Each one touches another, making them all joined together in perfect unity. Only by joining ourselves to Christ and to others, like the cherubim touching wings, do we pass through the "Levi Gate."

4. **Judah** means "to praise." Jesus Christ is the praise of Israel and the praise of every tender heart. As the Judah nature fills us, we begin to move into high praises. And we cooperate with our heavenly Lion in heavenly places as we execute his warfare tactics by leading the way with praise (Psalm 149). The word *Judah* also means "to hold out your hand" and "to throw or shoot a stone or an arrow at your enemy." In the book of Judges 1:1–12, Israel is preparing for battle as they move into the fullness of their inheritance, and they inquire of the Lord, "Who will be the first to go up and fight for us against the Canaanites?" In other words, who is it that will lead us in battle? The Lord answers them, "Send Judah (praise) first!" We fight our battle with praise. When we praise before the victory, we are demonstrating the highest level of faith. Judah got his name when his mother, Leah, chose to praise the Lord no matter what. We become warring priests as we move through the "Judah Gate."

5. **Zebulun** means "habitation" or "honor" (Ephesians
2:19–21). Jesus Christ is our habitation, our dwelling
place, the very dwelling place of God. And we, the
church, are the temple that the tabernacle pointed to.
All glory and honor belong to him. As the Zebulun
nature fills us, we, too, will be built together and
established as his glorious habitation on earth. Our
innermost being is God's temple, and collectively,
we become the habitation of God in the earth. The
local church is to be set apart as a holy dwelling place
that honors God in all things. As we pass through
these twelve stages of our sonship, we will become a
Zebulun people, his habitation. We don't just receive
things from God; we become his dwelling place, his
holy of holies on the earth. On our way to becoming
the New Jerusalem, we must pass through the
"Zebulun Gate." And we will experience the burning
presence of God in our midst (Zechariah 2:5).

6. **Issachar** means "there is a reward." When Jesus
comes, he brings his reward with him, for he is the
reward (Genesis 15:1). He is the fruit and reward of
the Father's heart. When we walk in this revelation,
our identity is secure and safe. He's not just our
crowning glory, but he is also our reward. All of life
points toward him. When we understand this, it
makes all of life come together, for then we are willing
to do anything he asks. Even the lowliest act of service
will be a joy when he is our reward. Every obedient
son and daughter of God will receive an indescribable

inheritance full of blessings (Ephesians 1:3; 2 Peter 1:3–4). When we pass through the "Issachar Gate," we joyfully discover that our union with Christ brings great reward—more of God (Hebrews 11:6).

7. **Dan** means "he has vindicated" or "judge." Everything about Jesus was a vindication of heaven. Our King refused to vindicate himself. Instead, he waited on the Father's honor to be released upon him first. Humility becomes the basis of true authority to judge. Jesus is our judge because he allowed the Father to be his vindicator. We have to give him our full heart, our everything, and allow him to be our vindication. There are seven judgments mentioned in the Bible: (1) *The judgment of sin on the cross* that eliminates the guilt and power of sin (Romans 6:23; 2 Corinthians 5:21; Hebrews 8:12). (2) *Judging ourselves* (1 Corinthians 11:31–32; 1 Peter 4:17). (3) *The judgment of Israel* (Zechariah 13:8–9). (4) *The judgment of the gentile nations* (Joel 3:1–2; Matthew 25:31–46). (5) *The judgment of fallen angels* (1 Corinthians 6:3; 2 Peter 2:4; Revelation 20:10). (6) *The judgment seat of Christ* (1 Corinthians 3:10–15; 4:5; 2 Corinthians 5:10). (7) *The great white throne judgment*, also known as the final judgment of the unbelievers (Revelation 20:11). To judge with true discernment is an act of righteousness. Discernment comes from the well of righteousness that belongs to God. The virtues of heaven are required to judge. One day, we will judge angels (1 Corinthians 6:2–3). To walk through the

"Dan Gate" implies that one has true discernment, perfect righteousness, love, and humility.

8. **Gad** can mean "good fortune" or a "troop." Who has been blessed with more favor and good fortune than our Prince of Glory? His armies of disciples are like a troop that marches with him in love. As he came out of the tomb on resurrection morning, you and I were transferred from death to life and became part of his fortunate troop of souls set free. He has taken us captive and seated us on high with him. He is the Firstborn of many brethren, and we are a troop that walks in his image. Jesus became a "troop" of passionate disciples that now exists in every nation of the world. One became many. Your life is meant to multiply into others as well. The favor and good fortune of grace empowers you to impart blessings to others. All of this will be seen as you walk through the "Gad Gate."

9. **Asher** is the Hebrew word for "happy one" or "righteous one." To go through the ninth gate on the way to the New Jerusalem, you will experience a glorious contentment in every circumstance that fills the heart. This is worship at its essence. Worship is being fully content in everything in Christ. There is no one filled with more joy than our Lord Jesus. Even on the cross, he endured all things for the "joy that was set before him." Our rejoicing Lord releases a divine happiness that cannot be described. It overcomes

difficulties with a laugh and deep sorrow with a song. Jesus satisfies our soul. He is fresh bread to the heart of every believer. Everyone who is righteous in Christ has the inheritance of Asher. Have you passed through this "Asher Gate"?

10. **Naphtali** can mean "wrestle" or "my struggle." To be free, Jesus wrestled with the forces of darkness throughout his life and ministry. Eventually, it led him to a garden called Gethsemane (olive press), where he prayed until he sweat drops of blood. Jesus wrestled with dark forces in order to purchase our salvation. We, too, wrestle at times with our own nature, our misdeeds, our attitudes, and relationships. Jacob wrestled with a man at midnight and received a blessing and a name change. He transformed inwardly from a "heel-grabber" to a "prince with God." This midnight wrestling man is living in you, and he will win. When he wins, you pass through the "Naphtali Gate."

11. **Joseph** means "may he add (another)." As we walk with our heavenly Joseph, blessings upon blessings come to us daily, loading us down with an eternal weight of glory. There will be no need or want when this Prince lives in your thoughts and in your spirit. When you feel like you can take no more, he will add yet another helping to your plate. The Father is seeking worshipers whom he can transform into the likeness of Christ. In a sense, God will "add another";

God will Joseph you. You will experience the fullness of his life as you pass through the "Joseph Gate."

12. **Benjamin** means "son of my right hand." At last, the fullness of the patterned son, Christ Jesus, is seen in his people. The Benjamin company will come forth as sons of power and sons of his glory. Seated at the right hand of God, the ascended ones will show forth his life for endless ages. Jesus is the true Son of God's right hand, but he has chosen us to be seated together with him (Ephesians 2:6; Revelation 3:21). The Benjamin company is a left-handed people, for they grasp the Father's right hand as they stand together. Ehud, a Benjamite, was left-handed, and God used him to bring deliverance. And there were seven hundred left-handed Benjamites who were so skilled as warriors that they could sling a stone with their left hands and not miss by a hairbreadth (Judges 20:15–16). The apostle Paul was also a Benjamite. He was one of the greatest teachers of the truth of sonship (Romans 1:11; Philippians 3:5). Taking God's hand with your left makes you a son of his right hand. How wonderful it will be as we pass through the "Benjamin Gate" and become the bridal company coming out of heaven like the New Jerusalem, the dwelling place of God.

Jacob had twelve sons and when their names are put together as they appear on the breastplate, we see a picture of the message of the gospel revealed. It's amazing how God hid all these wonderful truths in simple names and stories.

Reuben—Behold a son is born to us

Simeon—One who hears

Levi—Attached

Judah—Praise the Lord

Dan—He judged

Naphtali—My struggle

Gad—Good fortune

Asher—Happiness

Issachar—Reward

Zebulun—Honor

Joseph—Add to my family

Benjamin—Son of righteousness

This is what it says when compiled together:

Behold, a Son is born to us, one who hears us and who is attached to us. Praise the Lord. He judged our struggle and brought us good fortune, happiness, reward, and honor, and he added us to his family and called us sons of righteousness, sons and daughters of his right hand!

PICTURES OF JESUS IN JOSEPH'S LIFE

The life of Joseph gives us one of the clearest and most vivid pictures of the Lord Jesus Christ in the Bible. There is no one else in Scripture like Joseph, whose life points us to Jesus. It's like reading a preview of what Jesus would be like. There are so many fascinating parallels to Jesus embedded in the story line. Here are fifty comparisons between Joseph and Jesus Christ.

1. The meaning of Joseph's Hebrew name: Joseph means "adding" or "may he add." Adam was the great "subtractor," but Jesus, the last Adam, is the great "adder." Through the sacrifice made for every one of us, he gave us the opportunity to come in to his eternal family. Everyone who is saved is added to

heaven's number. And the Father adds to the church daily those who are saved in Jesus' name. He added us to the body of believers at our salvation. And he adds dignity, purpose, and meaning to our lives. Joseph's name points us to Jesus and shows us that God not only added salvation to us but also added to us every spiritual blessing in Christ (Ephesians 1:3).

2. The meaning of Joseph's Egyptian names: Joseph had two names, the name his mother gave him and the name the Egyptians gave him. His Egyptian name was Zaphenath-Paneah, which means "revealer of secrets" or possibly "God speaks through him and he (still) lives" (that is, God spoke through Joseph, and Joseph lived to tell about it!). Obviously, they gave Joseph that name because he was able to interpret Pharaoh's dreams and the dreams of his staff. Christ is the true "Revealer of Secrets" (Matthew 13:11), and God spoke through him, and he now lives forever in resurrection power. He is the revelator and the Great Revealer. Our Lord Jesus reveals what's going on in the hearts of men, and everything is revealed in his presence.

3. Joseph was a shepherd. Joseph fed his flock and cared for his father's sheep. And Jesus is the Great Shepherd of our lives (1 Peter 2:25), the Good Shepherd who guides (Psalm 23), and the Chief Shepherd, or Shepherd-King, who rewards (1 Peter 5:4).

4. Joseph was born to Jacob in his old age. Jesus was born on earth out of the eternity of the ages. From all eternity he was the Son of God. "In the very beginning the Living Expression was already there. And the Living Expression was with God, yet fully God" (John 1:1).

5. Jacob loved Joseph more than all his brothers. And so Father God loves his beautiful Son, Jesus. At his baptism, the Father's voice spoke, "This is the Son I love, and my greatest delight is in him" (Matthew 3:17).

6. Joseph wore a coat of many colors. This was a mark of honor and favor, and perhaps this multi-colored robe was a sign of the birthright. Jesus wore a seamless garment of righteousness. Revelation colors speak of Christ's virtues that surround him. Bright as the sun, glorious as the rainbow. Jesus has many colors, many virtues, many glories, and many perfections (Song of Songs 5:10–16).

7. The favor of Jacob and the rainbow-colored robe brought out the hatred of his brother's hearts toward young Joseph. Jesus likewise was hated because he exposed the wickedness of the hearts of men (John 3:19–20). Joseph's brothers wanted him dead, and so did Jesus' enemies. They wanted Jesus dead because he spoke the truth of God.

8. Joseph had a remarkable destiny. His dreams pointed him to the blessings that were yet to come. Each

dream was a divine announcement of his exaltation. And Jesus as well had remarkable announcements made about him before he was even born. It was even prophesied that the responsibility of complete dominion would rest upon his shoulders (Isaiah 9:6–7). Both Joseph and Jesus had remarkable destinies.

9. Joseph dreamed of an earthly exaltation. One of Joseph's dreams was of his brothers bowing down to him, and that dream was fulfilled when they came to buy food from him in Egypt. But this dream also points to the earthly reign that Jesus will one day experience. All his brothers (Jews) and gentiles will bow down to him and exalt his name (Philippians 2:9–10).

10. Another dream Joseph had involved the sun, moon, and stars bowing down to him. This pointed to the heavenly exaltation awaiting him. And Scripture says that Jesus was exalted above all his brothers and is now seated at the highest place (Ephesians 1:20–22). He is the Sovereign King, not only over the nations of the earth, but also over the kingdom of heaven. Both angels and the redeemed worship him (Revelation 4–5).

11. Joseph's brothers were envious of his dreams and the calling on his life. This caused his brothers to experience incredible jealousy. They couldn't stand to see their half-brother raised up over them. Jesus was anointed and favored by the Father. This infuriated

the Pharisees so much that they finally crucified him out of envy (Matthew 27:17–18).

12. Joseph's father sent him to see how his brothers were, but they didn't want him there (Genesis 37:12–13). Jesus was also a sent one. He was sent from heaven as God's servant with a divine commission. He came to his own, but they wouldn't receive him either (John 1:11).

13. Joseph's father sent him to see about his brothers from the Valley of Hebron, and he was thrown in a pit and left for dead. *Hebron* means "fellowship." Jesus was sent from heaven, a place of perfect fellowship with the Father (John 1:18), to taste death for every man (Hebrews 2:9).

14. Joseph's brothers were at Shechem when he arrived to check on them. *Shechem* means "shoulder." The meaning of *shoulder* is a place that bears burdens. Jesus came to bear the burden of the Father and of humanity. He bowed his shoulders and became a servant to all (Philippians 2:6–7).

15. Joseph was found wandering in the fields looking for his brothers who didn't want him (Genesis 37:15–16). The fields are a picture of the world (Matthew 13:38). Our Lord Jesus walked through the fields of the earth seeking the lost and caring for the needy. He told his disciples that the foxes had holes and the birds had nests, but he had nowhere to rest (Matthew 8:20). He

was looking for a resting place in the hearts of men but couldn't find it. Now his resting place is in the spirit of every believer (1 Corinthians 6:17).

16. Joseph found his brothers in Dothan. *Dothan* means "law" or "custom." And when Jesus found his people, they were all bound by the laws, customs, and traditions of their fathers (Acts 6:13–14).

17. Joseph's brothers hated him. And this jealous hatred caused them to plot. They wanted to take his life (Genesis 37:18). No sooner was Jesus born than the jealous hatred of him by the political powers of that day began to be displayed. Not only did Herod try to kill him, but the religious leaders of that day also discussed how they, too, might dispose of him (Matthew 12:14).

18. Joseph's words were not believed or valued by his brothers. They only hated him more for his words. They even ignored and despised his supernatural dreams. After Jesus was nailed to the cross, the people did not believe in him. They only reviled and mocked him, saying, "*If* you are the King" (Luke 23:37).

19. Joseph was stripped of his coat (Genesis 37:23). Jesus was stripped of his seamless garment (Matthew 27:27–28).

20. Joseph was cast into a pit. Jesus spent three days and three nights in the heart of the earth, or the pit of the earth (Matthew 12:40).

21. Joseph came out of the pit alive. Jesus came victorious out of his tomb leading captivity captive (Ephesians 4:8).

22. Joseph's brothers sold him into slavery with silver. Judas sold Jesus for silver. The Hebrew form of *Judas* is "Judah," the same name of the brother who sold Joseph.

23. Joseph's blood-sprinkled coat is shown to his father. Jesus' blood was taken within the veil before the Father (Hebrews 9:12). And his blood demonstrated to all of heaven that our sins were forgiven.

24. Joseph becomes a servant of others. He served Potiphar, and he served Pharaoh. Our heavenly Joseph, Jesus, came to earth not to be served but to serve. He came not to make a reputation but to give it all away in ministry for God and service to man (Philippians 2:5–12).

25. Joseph prospered, even as a servant (Genesis 39:2–3). Psalm 1 is a picture of the blessed man, Jesus, the One who prospers in everything he does. As a lowly, meek servant, Jesus prospered in all that he did.

26. Joseph's master was well pleased with him (Genesis 39:4). He walked in the fear of God and maintained

his integrity in all things. So it was with Jesus. He could say, "I only do that which delights his (the Father's) heart" (John 8:29).

27. Joseph was tested severely yet did not sin (Genesis 39:7–12). And in Jesus, the devil could find no foothold in his personality (John 14:30). He was pure, undefiled, and separate from everything unclean (Hebrews 7:26). Demons and men tested him, but he proved to be blameless.

28. Joseph was falsely accused (Genesis 39:16–18). And false witnesses, who spoke against Jesus at his trial before the Sanhedrin, also made false accusations about him, our Lord and Savior (Mark 14:53–67).

29. Joseph did not defend himself when he was accused (Genesis 39:19). And when Jesus faced false accusations, the Scripture says that he didn't open his mouth but was silent through it all. He never spoke out in anger or self-defense (Isaiah 53:7).

30. Joseph was cast into prison (Genesis 39:20). And our Lord Jesus Christ was unjustly condemned by Herod, sentenced by the Roman authorities, and cast into prison (Matthew 27:1–30).

31. Joseph suffered greatly at the hands of the gentiles (Psalm 105:17–18). Jesus was treated unfairly as the rulers and authorities gathered together against him

(Acts 4:26–27). He was mocked, spat upon, beaten, crowned with thorns, and nailed to the cross.

32. Joseph won the respect of the jailer (Genesis 39:21). As Jesus died, the Roman centurion testified that Jesus was a righteous man, the Son of God (Luke 23:47).

33. Joseph was imprisoned with two others (Genesis 40:1–3). Jesus was crucified between two thieves (Matthew 27:38), being numbered among the transgressors (Isaiah 53:12).

34. Joseph brought blessing to the one he was imprisoned with, the cupbearer, and pronounced judgment on the baker. Jesus took one thief into paradise with him, but the other thief mocked him and was left to die in his sins (Luke 23:39–42).

35. Yahweh revealed the future to Joseph through dreams. Jesus was the true prophet. He spoke from the Father's heart all that he was commanded to speak.

36. Joseph wanted to be remembered (Genesis 40:14). And the apostle Paul said that the disciples were to remember Jesus as they gathered around the Lord's Table, as Christ had asked them to do (1 Corinthians 11:24).

37. Joseph was delivered out of his prison (Genesis 41:14). He was not destined to live out his days there. Instead he was lifted out of the place of shame and was

given a seat of honor. And Jesus was laid in a tomb temporarily (Acts 2:24), but he, too, was lifted up to the place of highest honor and rests at the right hand of God.

38. Joseph was recognized as a revealer of secrets. The butler, the baker, even Pharaoh benefited from the divine insight granted Joseph. Even the wise men in the land weren't able to interpret the dreams of Pharaoh. It was the Father of heaven that revealed the mysteries to Joseph and gave him insight to interpret dreams. Jesus Christ walked in the anointing of the Spirit of revelation and knew the thoughts of men's hearts. His eyes were always on the Father so that he understood the mysteries of heaven (John 8:28; 12:49).

39. Joseph was a wonderful counselor to Pharaoh. He not only interpreted dreams, but he also gave strategic wisdom to the world leader. Joseph walked out the manifest wisdom of God. Christ, too, has been given the title wonderful Counselor. God sent him to impart wisdom to the rulers of the earth and to instruct all of mankind on how to come to the Father and be prepared for their future (Isaiah 9:6–7; Psalm 2).

40. Joseph was exalted from shame to glory. And he shared the throne of Pharaoh while our Lord Jesus Christ shares the throne of Father God.

41. Joseph received a new name. And God has highly exalted Jesus Christ and given him a name that is above every other name, Jesus, the Savior of the world (Philippians 2:9–10; Matthew 1:21).

42. Joseph took a wife, a gentile, in a foreign country. So our Lord Jesus purchased his bride from the nations of the earth by his death on Calvary (Revelation 5:8–10).

43. Joseph's two sons were named Manasseh, which means "forgetting," and Ephraim, which means "fruitful." Their names remind us of the forgiveness of our sin and of the way our heavenly Father *forgets* all of our sin because of the work of the cross through Jesus Christ our Lord. And because of what he did for us, we share in the *fruitfulness* of his life in us as true sons and daughters (Galatians 5:22).

44. Joseph was thirty years old when he began his life's work (Genesis 41:46). And Jesus was thirty years old when he began his public ministry (Luke 3:23).

45. Joseph's season of exaltation resulted in a season of abundant blessing for his family and all who came from all over the world, hungry and needing food (Genesis 41:47–49). And in Jesus Christ, all who hunger can come to him and feast. He will feed them living Bread (John 6:51). Our heavenly Joseph gives his bread to the hungry and perishing of this world

so that they might experience the abundance of life found in Christ Jesus our Lord.

46. Joseph was unknown and unrecognized by his brothers (Genesis 42:8). For years they believed Joseph was dead and gone, not realizing that God had sent him ahead to prepare the way for their deliverance. So it is with our Lord Jesus. His brothers (Israel) do not know him, but he has gone into heaven and will soon receive them as they bow before their Messiah King (Philippians 2:9–11).

47. Joseph saw, recognized, and knew his brothers (Genesis 42:7). Even though they didn't recognize him, Joseph's eyes were upon them. So the eyes of the Lord Jesus have been upon the Jews all through the long night of their rejection (Jeremiah 16:17; Hosea 5:3).

48. Joseph revealed himself to his brothers the second time they saw him. Stephen emphasized this in his parting message to Israel (Acts 7:13). The first time the brothers saw Joseph, they did not recognize him, but on their second visit to Egypt, Joseph revealed himself to them. The first time the Lord Jesus was seen by his brethren after the flesh, they knew him not, but when they see him the second time, he shall be known by them, and they will accept him as their Messiah (Revelation 1:7–8).

49. Joseph demonstrated tremendous grace toward his
    brothers. Joseph graciously wanted his brothers to
    come close to him, and then he kissed each one. He
    even encouraged them not to be grieved over what
    they had done or angry with themselves (Genesis
    45:4–5, 15). So shall it be when Israel is reconciled to
    Christ (Isaiah 54:7–8; Zechariah 13:1).

50. Joseph was a man of compassion and deep feelings.
    Seven times he wept. He wept when he listened to his
    brothers confessing their guilt (Genesis 42:24). He
    wept when he first saw Benjamin (43:30). He wept
    when he revealed his identity to his brothers (45:12).
    He wept as he reconciled with his brothers (45:15). He
    wept when he saw his father Jacob (46:29). He wept
    at the death of his father (50:1). And he wept when
    his brothers questioned his love for them (50:15–17).
    Jesus Christ was also tenderhearted and was often
    moved with compassion. We are told Jesus wept at
    least twice, once at the graveside of Lazarus (Luke
    11:22) and later over Jerusalem (Luke 19:41–44).

ENDNOTES

1 "The Impossible Dream (The Quest)," by Mitch Leigh, lyrics by Joe Darion, on Jack Jones, *The Impossible Dream*, Columbia, 1966.

2 Although we are not told exactly what the "bad report" might have contained, Joseph's brothers saw him as a tattletale and troublemaker. He may have exaggerated or slandered his brothers to his father.

3 Before the law of Moses, each family worshiped God with a chosen family member as priest, such as Eleazar (1 Samuel 7:1). As a prophet and a priest, Joseph was a striking picture of the Lord Jesus Christ, the one chosen of his Father to be a High Priest over the household of God. Another favored Son received the love and affection of his Father, the Son of Splendor, Jesus Christ! As the object of his Father's love (Proverbs 8:22), the One chosen for divine destiny was also

hated by his brothers. Joseph is one of the clearest types of Jesus found in the Scriptures. See Appendix 1.

4 In that day, twenty silver shekels was the going price to purchase a young male slave. See the Laws of Hammurabi, pars. 116, 214, 252, and Leviticus 27:5.

5 The text does not say with whom Potiphar was furious. Perhaps he knew his wife's promiscuous ways. He only had Joseph thrown into prison when a man with his authority could have had him killed. Perhaps he doubted the truth of her story, but to save face, he had Joseph imprisoned. According to the Yalkut Shimoni, Asenath, the daughter of Potiphar, did her best to convince her father of Joseph's innocence and what really happened. Later, when Joseph was freed from prison, Asenath became Joseph's wife.

6 Genesis 40:1. Eleven years passed since the time Joseph was sold into slavery. He was about twenty-eight at this time.

7 Genesis 40:1. Or "cupbearer" (literally, drink-giver). He was the king's trusted official who had a position to influence the king.

8 The love we never knew paid our debt at Calvary. Jesus put the "silver" of redeeming grace in our hearts. He provides for

us along the way. This chapter also furnishes us with a view of Jesus at the right hand of the Father who sees all and hears all yet loves us still.

9 Genesis 45:10. *Goshen* means "drawing near." It was a fertile area in the eastern part of the Nile delta that today is called Wadi Tumilat. It was known for grazing livestock (Genesis 46:32–34; 47:6, 11). Joseph's palace was apparently near Goshen.

10 Does this remind you of our heavenly Joseph? He was dead, but he lives! This tops Joseph! Our Savior is alive, and we will see his face.

11 Genesis 46:4. Within Jewish culture, even to this day, the nearest relative or oldest son would gently close the eyes of a loved one at death. Indeed, Joseph did as God had promised Jacob. See Genesis 49:33; 50:1.

12 The Septuagint translation of the Old Testament has seventy-five. See Acts 7:14.

13 The Levites became the priestly tribe and received no inheritance in the land. Instead they would live in forty-eight cities scattered throughout Israel (Numbers 18:20;

Deuteronomy 18:2; Joshua 13:33). And Simeon was eventually assimilated into the major tribe of Judah (Judges 19:1–9).

14   The words *future destinies* can also be translated "in the latter days."

15   Our Lord Jesus is the true Firstborn Son. He is the First Sign of the strength of heaven. How he excels them all in honor! How he surpasses others with his power! Worthy are you, Prince of Glory. All blessing and honor is yours forever. Your church is the Church of the Firstborn. Live in me, O glorious One.

16   See "Appendix 1, The Twelve Sons of Joseph."

ABOUT THE AUTHORS

Dr. Brian Simmons is a passionate lover of God. After a dramatic conversion to Christ, Brian knew that God was calling him to go to the unreached people of the world and present the gospel of God's grace to all who would listen. With his wife, Candice, and their three children, he spent eight years in the tropical rain forest of the Darien Province of Panama as a church planter, translator, and consultant. Having been trained in linguistics and Bible translation principles, Brian assisted in the Paya-Kuna New Testament translation project. After his ministry overseas, Brian was instrumental in planting a thriving church in New England (US) and currently travels full time as a speaker and Bible teacher. He is the lead translator of The Passion Translation®.

Candice Simmons is a true spiritual "mom" in the body of Christ. She is a mentor to many, both young and old. She was converted to Christ in the early 1970s and immediately began ministering to others. Candice is a prolific dreamer, experiencing many dreams each night for the last few decades. She is gifted to interpret dreams and has taught many classes and seminars on dream interpretation and "pastoring the prophetic." With a clear prophetic insight, she imparts love and wisdom to many churches. Her heart is fixed on blessing the emerging generation with a genuine passion for God.